More Mad for Miley

An Unauthorized Biography

by Lauren Alexander

PRICE STERN SLOAN
Published by the Penguin Group
Penguin Group (USA) Inc., 375 Hudson Street,
New York, New York 10014, USA
Penguin Group (Canada), 90 Eglinton Avenue East, Suite 700,
Toronto, Ontario M4P 2Y3, Canada
(a division of Pearson Penguin Canada Inc.)
Penguin Books Ltd., 80 Strand, London WC2R 0RL, England
Penguin Group Ireland, 25 St. Stephen's Green, Dublin 2, Ireland
(a division of Penguin Books Ltd.)
Penguin Group (Australia), 250 Camberwell Road,
Camberwell, Victoria 3124, Australia
(a division of Pearson Australia Group Pty. Ltd.)
Penguin Books India Pvt. Ltd., 11 Community Centre,
Panchsheel Park, New Delhi—110 017, India
Penguin Group (NZ), 67 Apollo Drive, Rosedale,
North Shore 0632, New Zealand
(a division of Pearson New Zealand Ltd.)
Penguin Books (South Africa) (Pty.) Ltd., 24 Sturdee Avenue,
Rosebank, Johannesburg 2196, South Africa

Penguin Books Ltd., Registered Offices:
80 Strand, London WC2R 0RL, England

Photo credits: Cover: courtesy of Albert L. Ortega/Prphotos.com; Insert photos: first page courtesy of Kevin Winter/Getty Images; second page courtesy of Frank Micelotta/Getty Images, Kevin Mazur/WireImage.com; third page courtesy of Frank Micelotta/AMA/Getty Images, F Micelotta/TCA 2008/Getty Images; fourth page courtesy of Jeff Kravitz/FilmMagic, Kevin Mazur/WireImage.com; fifth page courtesy of John Shearer/WireImage.com, Bryan Bedder/Getty Images; sixth page courtesy of Mike Marsland/WireImage.com, Jean Baptiste Lacroix/WireImage.com; seventh page courtesy of Steve Granitz/WireImage.com, Frank Micelotta/Getty Images; eigth page courtesy of K Winter/TCA 2008/Getty Images

Printed in the U.S.A.

Library of Congress Cataloging-in-Publication is available.

ISBN 978-0-8431-8928-5 10 9 8 7 6 5 4 3 2 1

More Mad for Miley

An Unauthorized Biography

by Lauren Alexander

PSS!
PRICE STERN SLOAN

Contents

	Introduction: The Best of Both Worlds	5
1	A Southern Star	7
2	Not Just Miley's Dad	13
3	Star Power	24
4	Disney Magic	30
5	So You Wanna Be a Pop Star?	39
6	Fame and Fortune	49
7	Los Angeles or Bust!	59
8	Mom (and Dad) Know Best	74
9	Chart Breaking	85
10	Here's Miley!	91
11	The Best Movie, Ever!	97
12	A Peek Backstage	102
13	Pretty As a Picture?	109
14	Breaking Out	114
15	Crushed	119
16	A Banner Year	124
17	The Most Important Role	134
18	The Sweetest Sweet Sixteen	139
19	Styling!	144
20	She's Got Music	155
21	A Perfect Five	160
22	A New Name	166
23	Pop Star	169
24	Fifty Fast Facts	174
25	Pop Quiz	179
26	Miley Mania	183
27	What's Next?	185

Introduction

The Best of Both Worlds

Thousands of screaming girls, with their moms and dads, are packed into the arena, along with a few boys. They are all there to see their favorite singer, and there isn't an empty seat in the house. Everyone has filed into their seats and the tension is mounting. When will the concert begin?

At last, the lights dim. A unified chant rises from the crowd: *"Hannah! Hannah!"* Then an announcer's voice says, "Are you ready for Hannah Montana?" The crowd cheers some more, waving their glow sticks in the air. From behind the screen, a silhouetted girl starts to sing. Then she appears—Hannah Montana! She's wearing a silver sparkly sweater set, black sparkly leggings, and boots. The aptly titled song "Rock Star" that Hannah sings sets the crowd into a frenzy!

The show is a blast, with Hannah working it hard on stage. And there's even a guest appearance by the heartthrob boy-band the Jonas Brothers.

But wait—there's more! Just when you thought the concert was over, the announcer says, "Are you ready for Miley Cyrus?" And there she is, rising from the stage floor—it's Miley's turn to rock the house. And she's *awesome*!

Chapter 1

A Southern Star

On November 23, 1992, a little star was born in Nashville, Tennessee. Her parents named her Destiny Hope because they thought she would go on to do great things. Boy, were they right! Her mom and dad, Billy Ray and Leticia "Tish" Cyrus, were probably very proud and happy parents. Billy Ray was a chart-topping country music star, and, at the time, he was basking in the glory of his mega hit "Achy Breaky Heart." Having an adorable baby girl only added to his joy.

Baby Destiny was happy, too—and very smiley. Her father loved her smile so much that he nicknamed her Smiley, which was soon shortened to Miley. And the nickname stuck. Her family, teachers, and friends all called her Miley—most people didn't even know her name was

Destiny! Since then, Miley has legally changed her name to Miley Ray Cyrus. According to E! Online, Miley's parents filed the name change petition on March 14, 2008 in Los Angeles Superior Court. In the petition, Miley's parents wrote, "Destiny Hope Cyrus has been commonly known as Miley Cyrus since she was a young child. The change of name is requested to make her commonly used name the same as her legal name."

Miley grew up in Franklin, Tennessee, a city just outside of Nashville with a very interesting history. Franklin was founded on October 26, 1799, and was named after Benjamin Franklin. For most of its first 180 years, Franklin was a very quiet city. But then the Civil War came, and the city was devastated. The Battle of Franklin, which was fought on November 30, 1864, was one of the bloodiest battles of the Civil War. It took a very long time to rebuild the city, but today, it is one of the wealthiest cities in Tennessee. In fact, it is one of the wealthiest cities in all of the United States.

With its close proximity to Nashville, the epicenter of the country music scene, Franklin attracts a lot of visitors. People living in Franklin have the best of both worlds! The city is a combination of small-town charm and big-city sophistication. If you were to visit Franklin, you could see some cool Civil War sites and museums, and gorgeous antebellum and Victorian homes. Plus, there is tons of shopping. Being a self-described "shopaholic," you can bet that Miley loves that feature of her hometown!

Probably because Franklin is so close to Nashville, several singers have decided to settle there. Josh Gracin, the fourth-place finisher on the 2003 season of *American Idol*, lives in Franklin with his wife and children. Carrie Underwood, *American Idol*'s fourth champ, lives there, too. And the pop-punk/emo band Paramore hails from Franklin as well.

Growing up in Franklin, Miley had a very happy childhood. She lived there with her big family: mom; dad; older half brothers, Christopher and Trace; older half sister,

Brandi; younger brother, Braison; and younger sister, Noah Lindsey. Needless to say, the Cyrus household was one busy place with all those kids running around!

Miley also had lots of pets. She had three dogs, two cats, and seven horses. Braiding her horses' tails was one of Miley's favorite things to do, and it's something she misses very much since moving to Los Angeles. After all, you can't keep all those horses in Tinseltown!

Miley's younger years were pretty normal—except for the fact that her dad was a huge country singer! According to the UK publication *Times Online*, one of Miley's earliest memories is of being onstage with her dad at an Elvis Presley tribute concert, and being held by star performers like Aretha Franklin.

Before she became a star, Miley attended Heritage Middle School, a Franklin public school with regular students and teachers. These days she has a private tutor, since there's no time to commute to a school. Having a private tutor is perfect for Miley's lifestyle since the tutor can go with her wherever she goes to give Miley her lessons. In school, math and creative writing were among Miley's favorite subjects. She's already put those creative writing lessons to good use, having penned over one hundred songs!

When Miley was in school, she loved to sing and dance. She had dreams of someday making it to Broadway. To get some performing experience under her belt, Miley decided to audition for the cheerleading squad and the dance team. In fact, one of Miley's most embarrassing moments happened when she was about to try out for the dance team in elementary school. She was wearing a jean skirt that day and, probably because she was so excited for the tryouts, she started dancing in the school's hallways. In the middle of a move, Miley slipped—and the skirt ripped! Miley turned bright red. Even though the guidance counselor was able to fix her skirt, Miley's mom was called, which only added to her embarrassment!

Being the children of Billy Ray meant that the

Cyrus clan got a lot of attention, but that proved to be good training ground for all the attention that was soon to come Miley's way. Not only is Miley following her dad's path to stardom, but so is her little sister, Noah. Born on January 8, 2000, little Noah Lindsey already has a lot on her acting résumé. She has appeared in five episodes of her sister's show, *Hannah Montana*. In "It's a Mannequin's World," Noah plays a little shopper. In "Oh Say, Can You Remember the Words?" she's a little girl on the beach. In "Torn Between Two Hannahs," Noah plays a little girl again. And in "Money for Nothing, Guilt for Free," she plays the role of a little girl in a ball pit who pinches both Lilly (as Lola) and Miley (as Hannah). Noah also appeared in six episodes of her father's television show *Doc*, playing Gracie Hebert.

Billy Ray must be mighty proud of his little girls!

Chapter 2

Not Just Miley's Dad

Up until *Hannah Montana* hit television, Billy Ray had always been known best for his hit single, "Achy Breaky Heart." It was a seriously catchy tune, but it was also the song that really started the line dancing craze. But if you ask anyone under the age of sixteen today who Billy Ray Cyrus is, they'd answer: "Miley's dad!"

Billy Ray was born on August 25, 1961, in Flatwoods, Kentucky. Flatwoods is what you would call a "bedroom community," meaning that there is no big industry or business in that town. It's what some people call a commuting town—you work in one town and live in another. Flatwoods is a quiet, safe, little town—ideal for raising a family.

Interestingly, Flatwoods was not the city's original

name. It was first called Advance, after the Advance Methodist Church. The name was later changed to Cheap, after John Cheap, the Methodist minister—but face it, who would really want to live in a place called *cheap*? In 1938, the city was renamed Flatwoods and has kept the name ever since. Flatwoods is a pretty good name for the place, since there was an area of flat, wooded land that ran through the city, parallel to the Ohio River.

Billy Ray had a lot of family around him when he was growing up. His paternal grandfather was a Pentecostal preacher. His father, Ronald "Ron" Ray sang in the gospel group, the Crownsmen Quartet. Billy Ray's maternal grandmother was a hoedown fiddler, and his mother, Ruth Ann, played bluegrass piano. It's easy to see where Billy Ray got his musical talent from.

Billy Ray's parents divorced when he was about five years old. Besides being a singer, his father was a popular Democratic politician. In 1975, Ron was elected to the Kentucky House of Representatives. Ron Cyrus served eleven consecutive terms—a total of twenty-one years. He finally retired from politics in 1996. On February 28, 2006, Ron Cyrus died from lung cancer. It was probably very hard for Miley to say good-bye to her grandfather. In honor of his memory, Miley has gravitated towards charity projects that help kids with cancer.

When he was growing up, Billy Ray dreamed of becoming a baseball player. In fact, he attended Georgetown College in Kentucky on a baseball scholarship, fully intending to carry out this dream. But then he bought a guitar and a new chord was struck. Billy Ray was hooked. He practiced like crazy and soon formed a band called Sly Dog with his brother Kevin.

Billy Ray loved playing in the band so much that he decided to ditch his baseball-playing dreams. However, he was realistic about the music industry, so he gave himself ten months to find a gig. As luck would have it, one week before his self-imposed deadline, the group got a call to be the house band for a club in Ironton, Ohio. They stayed there for two years, until a fire wiped out the bar—and all of Billy Ray's equipment!

But Billy Ray didn't give up. Instead, he moved to Los Angeles to pursue his music career. He quickly learned, however, that L.A. was no place for a country singer, so he headed back home. Based in Kentucky, Billy Ray commuted to the place all country crooners try to break into—Nashville! In Nashville, he tried to play gigs, desperately hoping someone would hear his music and sign him to a record deal. Luckily, someone *did* hear Billy Ray. It was a Grand Ole Opry star named Del Reeves who introduced Billy Ray to Harold Shedd of Mercury Records. And in the summer of 1990, Billy Ray signed a deal with Mercury.

Within two short years after inking his deal, Billy had a hit. "Achy Breaky Heart" sold nine million copies and spent seventeen weeks on the top of the charts—a record that's yet to be broken. (But watch out, Dad, Miley might give you a run for your money someday!) Billy Ray had women swooning at his feet. With his famous "mullet" haircut—

short in the front, long in the back—and a sculpted body, Billy Ray had to *fend* off the fans with his guitar (well, not literally!).

Even though Billy Ray's first album, *Some Gave All*, (from which "Achy Breaky Heart" was a single), was a mega success, he had a hard time following it up—a *really* hard time. Some say that part of Billy Ray's success was due to his hunky looks and part was due to the catchy tune of "Achy Breaky Heart." Whatever the formula, he could never replicate it, and the music world soon forgot poor Billy Ray.

In 1993, Billy Ray came out with the album *It Won't Be the Last*. It hit the charts at number three but fell way short of expectations. When *Storm in the Heartland* came out in 1994, it reached gold but was basically snubbed by the country music stations. And when Billy Ray tried to come back with *Trail of Tears* in 1996, his audience had dwindled even further.

Some people might have been totally devastated by

this "failure," but not Billy Ray. He soon found out that he had another talent—acting. "I was just kind of doing it as a hobby—just something to do—but I sure wasn't taking it very seriously," Billy Ray recalled. "I didn't take it seriously until a few years later when I had a chance to go in and audition for David Lynch's *Mulholland Drive*. David hired me, and it was during the process of filming *Mulholland Drive* that he pulled me to the side and said, 'I'm not your agent and not your manager, so I have nothing to gain from this. But I just want to tell you as a director that you could be a very good actor if you want to do that.'"

Billy Ray had also been following the careers of two singers, Dolly Parton and Kenny Rogers. He saw that they kept on working to achieve their dreams, even when radio stations were no longer giving their music a lot of airtime. How did they do it? They'd turned to acting.

Taking his cue from his fellow singers, Billy Ray hit the big screen. After filming *Mulholland Drive*, Billy Ray received a script for a TV show called *Doc*. Billy Ray read the script, liked it, auditioned, and landed the title role! From 2001 to 2004, Billy Ray played Dr. Clint "Doc" Cassidy, a Montana doctor who takes a job in a New York medical clinic.

But Billy Ray's love for music never left him. "Making music comes as naturally to me as taking a breath. It's what I do. Acting is something that I'm constantly trying to learn, every time I take the floor." In fact, Billy Ray wrote most of his new album, *Wanna Be Your Joe*, which was released July 18, 2006, while filming *Doc*. Billy Ray wrote or cowrote all the songs on the album, which he describes as "my most personal album yet." On the album, Miley joins her dad for one of the tracks—"Stand."

When the reviews came in, it was clear that Billy Ray still had what it takes. People loved it! Countrystarsonline.com summed up the reviews nicely: "Forget the mullet. Forget the push and pull of a line dancing train. Forget the past. Making music with lasting meaning, not for notoriety and not for quick passing chart success, is where this average Joe now finds himself. And there are many who couldn't be happier." Billy Ray was pretty happy, too!

Billy Ray thought he had enough of acting, and he had returned to music. Then along came *Hannah Montana*. Miley was cast first in the series, and then they cast her dad. "This is Miley's thing," Billy Ray told the *New York Daily News*. "She's worked too hard on it, and I didn't want to be responsible for her getting it or not getting it. I didn't want to come in and mess up her show. I've never done comedy and the last thing I want to do is ruin her show." Don't worry, Dad—you haven't messed things up at all!

But getting the part as Miley's dad on *Hannah Montana* didn't come so easily for Billy Ray. He had to audition—just like everyone else! "I was as nervous as can be," Billy Ray told the *New York Daily News*. "Miley came in and read the scene with me. And then they sent me out and, you know, I sat out in the lobby for a little while. And then they called me back in and I read it again. And then they sent me on my way."

Of course, Billy Ray got the job. "They just loved the chemistry between me and my dad," Miley told the *New York Daily News*. "It was great, just awesome." On the show, Billy Ray plays Robbie, Miley's father and manager. The part of Robbie is loosely based on his real life. In the show, Robbie is also a famous singer who doesn't really sing anymore. Sound familiar? The footage of Robbie as a famous singer is actual footage of Billy Ray himself!

Starring on a Disney Channel show has also brought Billy Ray a whole new slew of fans. A few days after the song "I Want My Mullet Back" aired in the "On the Road Again" episode, Billy Ray performed it in a concert. "I looked out and there were all these kids with mullet wigs in the audience," Billy told OCALA.com. "They held up signs saying, 'Billy, get your mullet back.'" Billy Ray's mullet song, which is on his new CD, is also played at sports arenas, especially during National Hockey League games. Mullets are called "hockey hair" because a lot of great hockey players had mullet haircuts. These days, Billy Ray is inundated with calls from the National Hockey League to sing the National Anthem at their games!

In 2007, Billy Ray got a call to be on one of the most popular reality-competition shows around: *Dancing With the Stars*. On the show, where stars are paired with professional dancers, Billy Ray took to the floor with Karina Smirnoff. Billy Ray will forever be remembered for his unconventional "Bubba Chicken" jive and "Hillbilly Waltz." Billy Ray and Karina were the seventh couple eliminated from the competition. Even though he didn't take home the big prize, Billy Ray had a great time on the show. "I do want to say thanks to all the fans. You've been awesome," Billy Ray said upon his departure from the show. "This has been a great experience."

Billy Ray's experience on the show was wonderful, and so was his exposure. Playing Miley's dad on *Hannah Montana* definitely increased Billy Ray's popularity. So Walt Disney Records pushed the release of his album

Home at Last up a month to July 24, 2007. The album was an immediate success, selling roughly 30,000 copies in its debut week and hitting number 3 on the charts. Billy Ray's music career was back and better than ever!

In 2008, Billy Ray took part in the Disney collection *Country Sings Disney* with two songs, "Ready, Set, Don't Go" and "Real Gone" (written by Sheryl Crow). "Real Gone" was also made into a music video that was widely played on CMT.

But even though Billy Ray's career is back on track, he's happy to let Miley take center stage these days. "Miley used to be known as Billy Ray Cyrus's daughter," Billy Ray told the *New York Daily News.* "Now I'm known as Miley Cyrus's father."

Chapter 3

Star Power

Miley had star power from the very beginning, and she was stagestruck at an early age. "I was singing on the stage with my dad when I was two," Miley told the *San Diego Union-Tribune*. "I would sing 'Hound Dog' and silly songs for the fun of it."

Although singing corny songs with her dad did not land her a record deal, those early performing days certainly made her feel comfortable singing in front of an audience. This early training helped make Miley into the secure, outgoing, fun girl we all know and love today. And Miley got a lot of practice writing songs with her dad, too. "Since Miley was a little girl, we've been writing songs together," Billy Ray told the *Associated Press*.

But all that singing didn't make Miley into an

immediate pop star. Remember that when Miley was just a tot, her dad was at the top of the charts. But then Billy Ray's music career waned, and he started to act. And guess what? Miley became interested in acting as well. Like father, like daughter.

Miley really began to get serious about showbiz when she was about nine years old. That was the time when her family moved from Franklin, Tennessee, to Toronto, Canada, where her dad was shooting the television series *Doc*.

Living in Toronto was a far cry from living in Tennessee. First of all, it gets very cold there! Toronto is the largest city in Canada; it's also the capital of the province Ontario. There are about 2.5 million people living in Toronto, making it the fifth most populated city in North America. As you can see, Toronto is much, much larger than Franklin, Tennessee! Miley was sad to leave behind her friends in Franklin, but she was also excited to move because Toronto is a very exciting city. Many films and television shows set in New York are actually filmed in Toronto because it looks a lot like the Big Apple. There's a large financial district with huge skyscrapers, and Toronto is known for its creative scene, including lots of theatre, art, and music. Of course, there's also lots of shopping!

When Billy Ray won the part of Clint "Doc" Cassidy in the television series *Doc*, it only made sense to move the family to Toronto, where the show was being filmed. *Doc* is the story of a handsome doctor from rural Montana who takes a job at Westbury Clinic, a small medical center in New York City. Clint's down-to-earth style and good bedside manner help him to win over his patients. Along the way, he faces challenges from other doctors on the staff and the medical system as a whole. Yet Clint manages never to lose his values.

Doc aired on the PAX network from March 11, 2001, through November 28, 2004. The show aired in the United States and more than forty other countries around the world. And in one of the shows—episode six of season four—Miley was a guest star. The episode, entitled "Men in Tights," originally aired on November 6, 2003. In that episode, she played a character named Kylie.

Even though Miley appeared on just one episode of her dad's show, she was hard at work going after her acting dream while they were in Toronto. "She was quite determined, diligent, and persistent," Billy Ray told the *San Diego Union-Tribune*. "While I was in Toronto, she found the best coaches, worked on her [acting] chops, went to auditions, and did all the different things to reach her goal." And Miley probably got the feel of what it would be like to be an actor from watching her dad. All those hours she spent on set as Dad filmed his TV show sure didn't discourage Miley from following her dream.

All of that preparation really paid off in 2003, when Miley appeared on the big screen in Tim Burton's flick *Big Fish*. Although the credits for the film cite her as Destiny Cyrus, it was definitely our Miley in the film! This PG-13 movie is the story of a son trying to learn more about his dying father by reliving stories and myths his father told him about himself. Miley had a very small part in the film. She played Ruthie, age eight. Miley was only on-screen for a few moments, but it gave her a taste of acting in a big project, and she instantly wanted more.

A few years later, when Miley was eleven, she auditioned for a Disney Channel show. The TV execs were looking for someone who had both acting and singing talent—the best of both worlds! "We decided we would not go through with this series until we found a kid who could carry a sitcom as well as she could carry a tune," Gary Marsh, president of entertainment for Disney Channel Worldwide, told *MusicWorld*. They auditioned a ton of girls who could act as well as Miley, but none of the girls could match her charisma. "I auditioned forever," Miley told *USA Today*. "At first they said I was too small and too young." Luckily for Miley—and for us—the network waited for Miley to grow up. In Miley, says Gary Marsh, "we saw a girl who has this natural ebullience. She loves every minute of her life. It shows in her demeanor and performance."

Disney knew they had their girl, so they offered her the biggest acting role of her life—Hannah Montana!

Chapter 4

Disney Magic

The Disney Channel has come up with a formula for success by making fantastic live action shows for kids and teens. They have a great track record of recognizing up-and-coming talent, and many stars including Britney Spears, Justin Timberlake, Hilary Duff, and Christina Aguilera, got their start at Disney. Disney also helped to boost the pop careers of *NSync, the Backstreet Boys, and Jessica Simpson through their televised concerts.

Disney definitely knows how to pick stars, but what really makes their shows successful is that they appeal to their viewers' imaginations. Take, for example, *That's So Raven*. This is the story of an average teenager, Raven Baxter. She goes through the typical trials and tribulations that every teen goes through—except for one twist—she has psychic powers. Now how cool would it be to have psychic powers? It's a fantasy that lots of people have. Everybody has secret wishes and fantasies, so shows that explore those are really fun to watch!

But fantasy aside, Disney Channel shows are so popular because they feature characters that kids can really relate to—characters that viewers would want to befriend. "The bottom line is you know you have good characters when kids go, 'Boy, wouldn't it be nice to hang out with them one day,'" Michael Poryes, the executive producer of *Hannah Montana* and *That's So Raven* told *USA Today.* "That's the secret, really, to the Disney Channel. We're more about the reality and the truth, what kids really go through: 'My friend is going to get dumped by this guy. What am I going to do?'"

The Disney Channel has also been hugely successful with its made-for-TV movies like *The Cheetah Girls* and *High School Musical.* These movies combine great story lines set in high school with music. How genius! And the CDs from each of these movies have sold millions of copies and burned up the charts. Disney has had hits with its television shows including *That's So Raven*, *Lizzie McGuire*, and *The Suite Life of Zack & Cody*. But Disney wanted more.

Enter *Hannah Montana*. *Hannah Montana* is the story of fourteen-year-old Miley Stewart, a girl from Tennessee who moves to Malibu, California, with her widowed father, Robbie, and her brother, Jackson. Seems like your average teen story, right? Well, this teen leads a double life as international pop-sensation "Hannah Montana." How does Miley hide her identity as a pop star? Simple—she wears a blond wig as Hannah and is her "regular old self" as Miley. Okay, you have to suspend some disbelief, but it works! Most of the show centers on Miley trying to live her life as an average teen. It's full of laughs, angst, and drama—and of course, music! Miley, as Hannah, sings all the songs on the show. *Hannah*

Montana also has a message: Fame is not to be confused with real life. You can only be truly happy when you stay true to yourself. This is a great message, and it was one Miley could really get behind.

Let's rewind for a minute: Disney had a great concept, with a great message to boot. But finding the right girl to play the star took them a lot longer. Gary Marsh did the normal casting calls in L.A. and in New York, but they didn't find anyone to fit the bill. Marsh was determined to find someone who could act in a sitcom and sing, plus be what he calls a "relatable, accessible girl." Basically they were looking for someone who everyone would want as her friend, but who could also sing and act.

Then one day, a tape came in. It was a tape from an eleven-year-old Miley Cyrus from Tennessee. We all know that at this point in her life Miley had no real performing experience, but she had that acting bug rooted deep inside her. Miley told *Scholastic News* that she knew she wanted to act "by going to the set with my dad and getting to see the environment and how much fun, joy, and encouragement there is on the set. It's great seeing everyone working together as a team on the show. You are all together and you're all in a family, and it's a really great place to be." The execs asked Miley to perform in front of them. She walked into a room of fifteen people, undoubtedly with a big smile on her face and a ton of confidence. And then she sang. That was the first moment it crystallized that she was the "it" girl.

Even though Miley knew she wanted to act and even though Disney thought she was the best girl for the job, they were uncomfortable hiring someone so young. It didn't matter that her dad was a star. It didn't matter that she had raw talent. Disney wanted experience, and that was something Miley could not make up. Luckily, Disney waited. They put the show on hold until Miley grew up a little.

After Miley got involved, a few things changed on the show. Originally, the main character was called

Chloe Stewart and her pop star name was Alexis Texas. But Miley wasn't impressed with Alexis Texas. She was actually the one who suggested they change the name to Hannah Montana! But the Disney bigwigs were the ones that changed Chloe to Miley. When the UK publication the *Times Online* asked Miley why she thought this happened she said, "They just thought I was like the character (and) the character was so much like me—because she's really wild and fun and doesn't really give a care. And that's very much how I am. What you see is what you get. I'm not really worried about stuff, I just like to get stuff done." Miley continued by saying, "She doesn't wanna be something that's hot right now. She wants to go on forever."

And on and on Miley did go! The producers and network bigwigs loved Miley's acting skills. They felt that she was confident, but not cocky, and her comic timing was near genius. And they were also blown away by her husky-sounding singing voice. "She has the everyday relatability of Hilary Duff and the stage presence of Shania Twain, and that's an explosive combination," Gary Marsh told reporters.

Even though the execs were convinced that Miley was the "it" girl, they still had to sell her to their advertisers and, more importantly, to the viewers. So Disney put on a concert at the Alex Theatre in Glendale, California. The setup was this: A group of seven hundred kids and teens were invited to a concert, and were told that there was a chance to be on TV. A free concert plus the chance of being on TV—who could refuse that?

Miley had only four days to get ready. Feverishly, she worked with a coach and a choreographer to get six songs perfectly staged.

On the night of the concert, the place was packed. Miley's nerves were probably on edge, her heart racing. But when she hit the stage—as Hannah Montana—the crowd went wild! The reaction surprised everyone, especially Miley! "It was crazy because I was expecting dead silence," Miley said. "They had no idea who Hannah Montana was."

Disney had sold *Hannah Montana* to the viewers; now it was on to the advertisers. In early spring, television networks unveil their forthcoming seasons to advertisers. This is called "upfront." During the upfronts, TV executives have to convince the advertisers that their show will be a hit. Since advertisers want their commercials to be seen by a lot of people, it only makes sense that they'd want to hook up with a hit show. Lots of viewers equal lots of potential buyers of their products. A television show cannot really survive without its advertisers. It's all economics. Advertisers pay the networks for their commercial spots; the networks need this money to make a profit. Once the media buyers saw the Hannah Montana "concert," they were convinced that the show was going to be a hit, and they signed on.

That was a good move. *Hannah Montana* premiered on March 24, 2006, and was an instant hit! Granted, it got a bit of a push by being the lead-in to an encore showing of *High School Musical*, and by having Corbin Bleu (of *High School Musical* fame) guest star on the first episode. But in the end, the episode raked in 5.4 million viewers. Miley knew right away that *Hannah Montana* was a hit. "I was on Google every five seconds, getting Google Alerts! Same thing as I do for my records," Miley admitted to a reporter from the UK publication the *Times Online*.

Disney, Miley, and legions of fans knew that *Hannah Montana* was a hit, and that it was here to stay. Since then, in its regular time slot on Sunday evenings, *Hannah Montana* garners over 3.5 million viewers, making it the most popular show among tweens.

Disney's done it again!

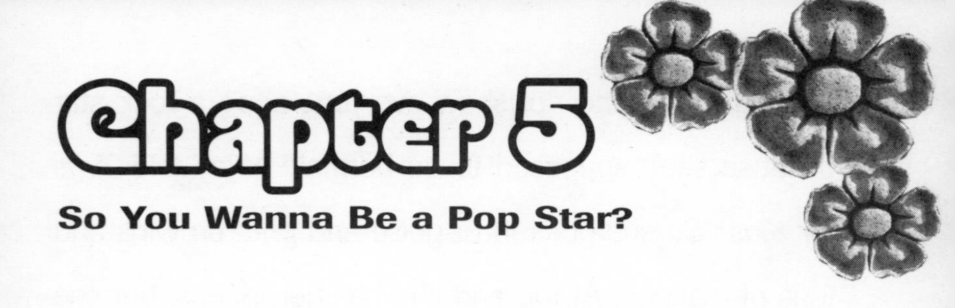

Chapter 5

So You Wanna Be a Pop Star?

It would be pretty cool to be a pop star, wouldn't it? Think of all the fame and fortune—the amazing things you could buy with the money you make, the incredible places you'd be able to jet off to. Think of the fans who would follow you around all the time—when you are eating, when you are shopping, when you are trying to relax. You'd have to be nice to your fans; you are obliged to give your autograph. After all, you're nothing without your fans, right? But it would be nice to have a little quiet time now and then.

The story of *Hannah Montana* is about having all the perks of a pop star, but still being able to live a normal life. "It's about a rock star who just wants to be with her friends and family and be a normal girl, and she tries to go in disguise and not show everyone she's a rock star because she's supposed to be normal," Miley told *Time for Kids*. "So she goes in disguise and puts on wigs and tons of makeup. At the end she has her friends, but she also has her secret life of being a rock star." But *Hannah*'s more than a show about a girl who leads a double life. The show has an underlying theme that lots of teens can relate to—wanting to be someone else, yet working hard to keep your own identity.

On the first episode of *Hannah Montana*, "Lilly, Do You Want to Know a Secret?" Miley Stewart has recently moved from rural Tennessee to snazzy Malibu, California. Miley Stewart is your typical fourteen-year-old kid, and she becomes best friends with a girl named Lilly. Everyone their age is just wild about pop star Hannah Montana, and they are all bummed when Hannah's concert is sold out. Then, Lilly scores two tickets, and she invites Miley to come along. The only problem is that Miley is really Hannah Montana. How can she be onstage and in the audience at the same time? Miley really doesn't want to spill her secret to Lilly, because she's afraid their friendship will change. Miley loves the relationship they have, but she's scared that if Lilly finds out her true identity, she'll treat her like a pop star and stop being the true friend she is. This is a dilemma that lots of teens can relate to. They want their friends to like them for who they are inside; they don't want them to like them, say, because their family has a lot of money, because they have a famous relative, or because of how they dress.

But when Lilly sneaks into Hannah's dressing room, she eventually discovers that Miley is really Hannah Montana. What a shock that is to Lilly! Lilly is really upset that Miley didn't tell her the truth—after all, they are best friends, and best friends are supposed to tell each other everything, right? In the end, though, Lilly and Miley make up, and Lilly agrees to keep Miley's secret.

Keeping secrets is something everyone can relate to. They are sometimes hard to keep, and we're always scared that somehow our secrets are going to be revealed. Having—and keeping!—secrets is part of growing up. There are secrets about who you are crushing on and secrets about whom your best friends are crushing on. There are secrets about presents you are buying and secrets about presents others are buying for you.

Some people are great at keeping secrets. Other people are, well, not so great at it. Miley Stewart and Hannah Montana are great at keeping secrets, but Miley Cyrus? Not so much. When asked about how the real-life Miley resembles the TV Miley, Miley told Girl.com.au: "The differences are easiest—I'm not very good at keeping secrets at all! If you want your secret kept, do not tell me! I'll be triggered by a memory and I'll just want to say what it is! Or I'll say to my mom, 'You will not believe what is happening!'"

But it's no secret that *Hannah Montana* has been a huge hit. The debut show drew Disney's highest audience ever for an original series. In fact in the 2006 season, among kids ages two to eleven, *Hannah* was right behind *American Idol* as the most-watched show.

Miley was psyched to have a starring role on such a popular show, and she has loved every minute of working on it. It has been really fun for Miley, but it has also been a lot of hard work. Not only does she have to put in long hours on the set, but she has to play two different parts! "To be able to stay in there and focused is the best thing you got to do," Miley told *KnoxNews*. One of Miley's favorite moments in the first season of the show was getting to work with country music star Dolly Parton. Miley has known Dolly for many years, but just as a friend of her dad's. (Billy Ray and Dolly had performed together on several occasions.) But now Miley was getting to work with her on a professional basis, and she was thrilled! On the episode, "Good Golly, Miss Dolly," Dolly Parton plays the part of Miley's aunt. Aunt Dolly gave Miley lots of advice about her love life and almost messed things up between Miley and her crush, Jake Ryan. Miley, who calls

Dolly "Aunt Dolly" in real life, had a great time getting to know Dolly better and they are now very close.

A thing like almost having your secret crush revealed is something that a lot of girls can relate to. In fact, most of the *Hannah Montana* episodes offer very valuable life lessons. Betcha that you've come across some of these situations in your life:

Unrequited love: In "Miley Get Your Gum," Miley's friend Oliver has a crush on Hannah Montana. Of course, Hannah does not feel the same way. Miley and Lilly try to talk him out of his crush, but no deal. So, Miley fesses up that she's really Hannah Montana. Crush over. But in season two's "Achy Jakey Heart" when Miley finally confesses her dual identity to crush Jake Ryan, he accepts her for who she is and the two become a couple.

Disobeying your parents: In "She's a Supersneak," Miley and Jackson desperately want to meet

Ashton Kutcher at his movie premiere. But Dad says they can't go. Not wanting to miss this opportunity, Miley and Jackson sneak out, only to later get caught red-handed by Dad!

Lying to your best bud: In "It's My Party, and I'll Lie if I Want To," Miley lies to Lilly about going to a party. But when the paparazzi nab Hannah Montana at the bash, Lilly finds out. Of course she's hurt, but in the end, the true friends make up.

Trying to play matchmaker: In "Oops! I Meddled Again," Miley and Lilly try to set Oliver up with a girl at school named Becca. But this is no easy setup, and things get more complicated as the girls meddle further into the lovebirds' business.

Being vain: In "You're So Vain, You Probably Think This Zit Is About You," Lilly has to wear glasses right before a big skateboarding competition, and Miley gets a big zit that shows up on her poster picture.

Forgetting that your best friend is more important than your crush: In "More Than a Zombie to Me," Miley turns down Jake Ryan's offer to go to the dance. But when Miley finds out that Lilly agreed to go with Jake, she decides to try to steal Jake away. She ends up really hurting Lilly, but eventually realizes that no boy should come between a girl and her best bud.

Sometimes we all neglect our school-work: In "Get Down, Study-udy-udy," Miley is so psyched about her upcoming European tour that she neglects her studies. In fact, her dad threatens that the tour will be cancelled if she doesn't pass her biology midterm. In the end, with the help of a song and dance routine (to help her memorize bio) and her friends, Miley passes with flying colors.

Miley came a long way, from her casting days to her starring role on *Hannah Montana.* "She was this short little scrawny girl with a raspy voice—she almost had the voice of a truck driver. It made her stand out," Adam Bonnett, senior VP of original programming for the Disney Channel, told *Variety.* And the producers of the show have let the character of Hannah Montana grow with Miley. When the writers of the show knew that Miley was excited to start driving when she turned sixteen, it "inspired writers to do a story [that] season where Miley Stewart goes to get her driver's license and fails," Bonnett explained. He continued by saying, "And she realizes that if she goes back as Hannah Montana, they'll give it to her because she's Hannah Montana—that's all inspired by Miley's passion for getting behind the wheel."

On the show, Miley has to jockey back and forth between Miley Stewart and Hannah Montana, which can become confusing at times! In real life, Miley's roles sometimes confuse her fans, too. They don't know whether to call her Miley or Hannah. After all, she is both girls, right? Well, sort of. The real person is Miley Cyrus. Hannah Montana is fictional. Yet, when Miley tours, she is Hannah, so she really doesn't mind when her fans call her that. Miley figures that fans probably call her by the name of the character they feel most comfortable with, or the character they can best relate to. If they like the sparkly, outgoing, performing type, then they call her Hannah. If they relate better to the girl-next-door type, the girl who just wants to fit in, they call her Miley.

Sometimes life can get a bit confusing for Miley. But one thing's for sure—she's a star!

Chapter 6

Fame and Fortune

When MediaVillage.com asked Miley Cyrus if she thought *Hannah Montana* was going to become really popular, Miley said, "I hope so. Hannah in the show is enormous, like a Hilary Duff of TV. I hope everyone really likes her. She's a great person." Well, Miley's "hope" certainly has come true. *Hannah Montana* is an enormous success. But how has life changed for Miley since becoming a mega star? Well, it's changed in lots of ways.

First of all, Miley and her family now live in Los Angeles. "Everything is completely different," Miley told *Discovery Girls* magazine. "I come from this really small town near Nashville, Tennessee, where everything was la-di-da and normal. And then, all of a sudden, everything is completely the opposite. I went from living in slow motion to living at two hundred miles an hour!"

You can say that again. L.A. isn't anything like Miley's hometown of Franklin, Tennessee. And even though Miley had a taste of city life when she lived in Toronto, nothing compares to L.A. Los Angeles is the most populated city in the state of California—there are over 3 million people living there! L.A. is the home to major cultural centers, science and technology industries, and, of course, it is the place where movies, TV shows, music, and careers are made.

Miley certainly made her career in L.A.! After Miley became so successful, the family decided that they needed more space—and privacy! So, in August of 2007, the Cyrus family moved into a Mediterranean-style mansion in a gated community. The house has five bedrooms, six bathrooms, a gorgeous kitchen, a formal dining room, a living room, a family room, a library, a screening room, and a gym.

Some people might think it's unfair that it was Miley's money that bought the family's gorgeous house. Other may think that this makes perfect sense. But Miley was more than happy to buy a house for her whole family. After all, without their support, she wouldn't have a career. And Miley's parents made sure that Miley has plenty of space in the new house—she has an entire suite of the house, complete with a bedroom and a separate sitting room, all to her self. It's where Miley "can just chill out," Tish told *People* magazine. In exchange, Miley has promised to live at home until she's 20. With that set up, who would want to leave?

"Our house is fun," Miley told InStyle.com. "Parts of it are really modern, but it's mostly old Italian country." When decorating her suite, Miley and Tish took their inspiration from the super cool Viceroy Hotel in Santa Monica. The suite has sea blue walls, and lamps filled with coral. Over Miley's bed hangs a lovely shell chandelier. "It feels beachy and Old Hollywood. I love the way the room is laid out," Miley said. The suite is a perfect place to crash after a hard day's work, and at the same time a perfect place to hang out with friends like Mandy Jiroux and Ashley Tisdale.

When Miley moved to L.A. and began the grueling schedule of filming a TV show, she had to give up going to public school. She now spends about three hours a day with a tutor in order to keep up with her studies. Miley told *Teen* magazine that absolutely everything has changed since she and her family moved to L.A. "Everything is so different because I'm from a small town and going from that to moving out to Hollywood—everything is completely opposite. It was hard but it's really cool that I'm able to live my dream and all of these things are happening to me."

Miley really realized just how much her life had changed when her little sister, Noah, told her that she had entered a contest on the Disney Channel website to win backstage passes to a concert featuring the network's newest star—Miley Cyrus. "You live with me!" Miley told her sister. And then, according to the *New York Times*, Miley warned her sister not to swipe anything from her room to sell on eBay!

A Miley Cyrus possession would probably go for big bucks on eBay. These days, fans are going wild just at the sight of her. "The last time me and my mom went [to the shopping mall], it turned out not to be such a good idea," Miley told MSNBC.com. "People rushed into the store we were in, and they had to shut the doors until everyone would go away. It was crazy."

Crazy, but true. Miley is now a *huge* star. But even though she's super popular now, Miley hasn't lost her down-to-earth charm or her Tennessean drawl. She's always greeting people with a "How y'all doing?" Miley is the kind of girl you'd love to have for a friend. She's loyal and honest and a lot of fun to be around. In fact, she's a lot like the character Miley Stewart she plays on TV.

When *Scholastic* asked Miley to describe Miley and Hannah, here's what she had to say: "Miley is just like me, but she's also like any other average girl going through love stuff, friend stuff, and family stuff. But she is trying to get through the pressure of being a universal superstar. Everyone loves Hannah, but she just wants to have her friends and her family."

Miley understands why fans idolize Hannah. After all, she has a few idols of her own: Beyoncé, the soulful lead singer of Destiny's Child and smokin' solo artist, is one of Miley's idols. Miley would love to have a career as amazing as Beyoncé's. Another star that Miley looks up to is Raven, the star of the Disney Channel's *That's So Raven*. Miley thinks Raven is a loving person—and totally funny, too! Miley is also a big Hilary Duff fan. In fact, Miley's entire family loves Hilary! Miley thinks it's very cool that Hilary started *Lizzie McGuire* at the same age Miley started *Hannah Montana*. "The way that I am doing the business and everything is kind of following in her footsteps," Miley told a reporter on the set of her show. "So watching her grow as a singer and an actress is helping me as well."

Miley does have one idol that most of her fans would never guess—Judge Judy! Miley totally freaked when she met Judge Judy! "She's my idol! I was like, 'Oh my goodness, what do I say to her? I'm so nervous! What if she thinks I'm so weird?'" But Judge Judy was perfectly nice to Miley and made her feel comfortable. After that encounter, Miley *really* knows how her fans feel when they meet her.

If you think about it, Miley Cyrus's life kind of mirrors the life of the character she plays on TV. Miley Cyrus is trying to get through the pressures of being a big star, yet she's still an average girl at heart. Miley still has to do things at home, like clean her room, make her bed, and load the dishwasher. And every Sunday, Miley goes to church with the rest of her family.

Of course, Miley isn't always perfect. Like lots of teens, she sometimes gets in trouble for talking back to her parents. "When I get home I'm really not in the mood to deal with my brother or little sister, and so usually I'm kind of snapping at them," Miley admitted to *Popstar!* magazine. Like a true teen, Miley insists that her behavior is not her fault—her siblings started it! And, like anyone else her age, Miley gets grounded when she does something wrong.

And that's okay with Miley because she really just wants to be treated like any other teen girl. She doesn't want fans to be afraid of her because she's a star. Miley, as Miley Cyrus the actress, doesn't have an alter ego to hide behind. And she never hides from fans because she loves meeting them. "I wouldn't want to be treated differently," Miley told *Girls' Life* magazine. "I wouldn't want to be someone you couldn't say hello to. I want to be very approachable. Say 'hi' to me. I love it." Miley wants all her fans to have a chance to take a picture with her or to have an autograph signed. So, the next time you see Miley, make sure you say hello!

However, there are times when having fans recognize her can be a little overwhelming. A few years ago, Miley could hang out at the mall or movies and maybe one or two people would notice her. Today, when Miley hits the streets, she's recognized instantly. There are no more quiet shopping days or relaxing trips to the movies for Miley. Once, she went to the Universal Studios theme park with her brother and a friend, and she was immediately recognized. "It was craziness," Miley told a reporter. "All the kids on every ride. I felt like I was going to hurl after one ride, and all the kids were like, 'Hannah Montana is about to puke!'" One thing is for sure: When you're a star, you have to be ready to sacrifice all sense of privacy.

Miley has had some weird experiences with fans. She told a reporter from *Time for Kids* that she gets lots of letters that say, "'Do you mind giving these letters to your friend Hannah Montana?' or 'Where's your friend Miley?' 'I'm like . . . it's all the same person!'" Apparently, some people think that Miley and Hannah are two separate people!

Most fans are psyched to meet Miley and would do anything for an autograph or a photo op. But there are others who are, well, downright rude. Miley told *Discovery Girls* magazine about a funny run-in she had with a fan: "I was having lunch with my brother, and I had on my pajamas. I wasn't wearing makeup, and my hair was totally nasty. So we get to the restaurant and the first thing I hear is, 'You look a lot better on TV.' Sometimes it's really weird to hear stuff like that. I just think, 'Well, that was harsh!' But then again there are times when someone will come up to me and say, 'Omigosh! You're so cute and I love your shoes.' And when that happens I just think, 'This is sweet!'"

Yes, life is certainly turning out to be very sweet for Miley Cyrus.

Chapter 7

Los Angeles or Bust!

Miley's move to L.A. brought mixed emotions. Sure, she was totally pumped to land the role as Hannah Montana, but getting that part meant that she and her family would have to move. When Billy Ray landed the part in *Doc*, the family's move to Toronto was more temporary. This move looked like it was going to be for real.

Moving to L.A. meant saying good-bye to her farm, to her animals, to her grandparents, and to her best buds. "It was bittersweet," Miley told *J-14* magazine. "I hung out with a small group of friends I've known all my life because I went to the same school my whole life."

Miley was especially going to miss her best friend, Lesley. Miley and Lesley had known each other since they were six years old. The pair did everything together. "I was used to seeing her every day and talking to her all the time," Miley told *J-14*. "Once I moved to L.A., I knew I wasn't going to see her at all." Lesley has always been a true friend to Miley, through and through! When Miley was going through the grueling audition process at Disney, Lesley was there to offer encouragement. When Miley was bummed about moving to L.A., Lesley was there to cheer her up, even though she was pretty bummed herself. Right before the big move, the best buds spent one last day together. The girls couldn't stop bawling at the thought of being separated. When Miley's mom came to pick her up, Miley told her that she didn't want to leave. Miley's mom was supportive and told her that she didn't have to make the big move if she didn't want to. But deep down inside, Miley knew that she had to go; if she didn't, she'd be giving up her dream of becoming a star.

Even though Miley lives two thousand miles away from her friends in Tennessee, she's managed to keep in touch with them—especially Lesley. In fact, Lesley made it out to L.A. to catch Miley's first big concert. "I realize now that you can't be afraid to lose people," Miley told *J-14* magazine, "and that's the thing I was afraid of the most. You can't lose somebody if you always hold on to them."

Moving is hard for anyone. You have to get used to a new city and a new house. You have to get used to a new school. But the hardest thing to do when you move is to make new friends. This is especially difficult when you are in middle school. By this time, most kids have already found their groups and breaking into a new clique can be next to impossible.

But Miley was lucky. Sure, she had to get used to an entirely new city and house, but since she was going to be working 24/7, she wouldn't be going to a normal school, so she wouldn't have to deal with the social pressures there. Also, Miley's not the type of kid to shrink into a corner and not talk to anyone new. Just the opposite—Miley's bubbly personality made it easy for her to fall in with the Hollywood set.

Miley has made a lot of new friends in Hollywood. One of her new buds is Ashley Tisdale. Miley even has a picture of them on the screen saver of her Sidekick. Some people have said that when Miley dons her blond wig, the two can pass for sisters! Making friends with other stars was really helpful for Miley because they really understand what each other are going through. Making friends who weren't stars was a little harder. Miley found out the hard way that when you're a big star, you have to be careful about who you're friends are. People can pretend to be your friends, and then turn around and sell your secrets to the tabloids for big bucks!

Luckily, Miley found a best friend in L.A. who works in the entertainment industry, but isn't a huge star herself. Her name is Mandy Jiroux and she has been one of Miley's back-up dancers. Mandy understands the pressures of working in Hollywood, and she isn't overwhelmed by Miley's fame, which makes her a perfect best bud. "I think you've got to keep a very close circle of people you can trust," Miley told *Seventeen* magazine. "I've had so much drama with girlfriends . . . Honestly, I can't think of one other friend I can trust like I trust Mandy. She's really the only person I can call and say anything to."

Miley and Mandy have become so close that they have their own show on YouTube—*The Miley and Mandy Show*. Most of the show, which is filmed for fun, takes place in Miley's bedroom in her family's home in Toluca Lake, California. On the show, the best friends dance, goof around, and have a great time together.

When *Teen* magazine asked Miley for her definition of a true friend, Miley said, "A true friend is someone who is always there during the ups and downs. I actually have a song called 'True Friend' . . . I have had a lot of positive things happen in my life, but I also have had some negative things that are not so fun to deal with . . . so it is nice to have my friends there to help me get through everything."

Miley has also been lucky to make friends on her show. She's become very tight with Emily Osment, who plays Lilly Truscott, and Mitchel Musso, who plays Oliver Oken. Miley has also become close with Jason Daniel Earles, who plays her older brother, Jackson.

In real life, Jason was born on April 26 in San Diego, California. The exact year of his birth is somewhat of a mystery. Some reports say 1985, while others list 1977. That's an eight year difference, and Jason's mum about the truth! Jason can be seen in the movie *National Treasure*, and he worked on *Phil of the Future*, playing the role of Grady Spaggett, an advanced math student.

When Jason first started working on *Hannah Montana*, he couldn't believe how well everyone got along. "This group got really tight, really quickly," Jason told *Popstar!* magazine. "By the end of the pilot, all the kids were like swapping numbers and staying over each other's houses and hanging out." Jason says that they all became so close that they started acting like a real family—complete with bickering. But not to worry—they always made up!

Even though Miley is cool with her on-screen brother, off-screen, she hangs out more with Emily and Mitchel. Costar Emily Osment plays Lilly Truscott, Hannah Montana's (and Miley Stewart's) best friend. Emily Jordan Osment is a California girl. She was born in Los Angeles on March 10, 1992. Living in the land of the stars, acting was in the air. It was also in her blood: Her dad, Eugene Osment, is an actor, as is her older brother, Haley Joel Osment (of *The Sixth Sense* fame).

When Emily was five years old, her dad asked her if she wanted to get into the biz. Emily started doing commercials and in 1999, she landed her first film, *The Secret Life of Girls.* Following this, Emily appeared in Hallmark's *Sarah, Plain and Tall: Winter's End.* Other TV work included *3rd Rock from the Sun, Touched by an Angel,* and *Friends.* Then in 2002, she landed the role of Gerti Giggles in *Spy Kids 2: Island of Lost Dreams.* When writer-director

Robert Rodriguez saw Emily audition, he was so blown away by her performance that he wanted to give her more screen time, so he made her role in the film longer! Emily then went on to star in *Spy Kids 3-D: Game Over.*

With such an impressive résumé, you'd think that Emily would've had no problem landing the part of Lilly. There's no way she'd have to wait as long as Miley did for her part. Well, the role didn't come so easily to her. She had to audition about three or four times. At her last audition, when Miley was already cast, they had Emily read with Miley. The two obviously had some chemistry, and Emily won the part!

Emily admits that she had no idea that *Hannah Montana* would become such a hit. When she first landed the part, she thought she was going to be part of a cute show, something that would quietly air on the Disney Channel. Even after they shot the pilot, and people were gushing at how great it was, Emily was not fazed. Boy, was she surprised at the way things turned out!

When Emily first started filming *Hannah Montana*, she would have never guessed that she'd soon be recognized by fans as soon as she stepped out her door. True, when the show first hit, people would approach her and ask if she played Lilly, but now when fans see her, there's no doubt who she is!

When TheStarScoop.com asked Emily how she and Lilly were alike and different, here's what she had to say: "I think I'm most like Lilly because I really like to do sports. She's a really sporty girl. She likes to get on her skateboard . . . She's really out there and social, and that's sort of like me, too. And I think the way I'm sort of not like Lilly, is, she has . . . the coolest clothes I have ever seen . . . I would love to have those kind of clothes."

Both Emily and Miley like to shop. Emily told *Popstar!* magazine that she likes to shop at stores like Abercrombie & Fitch and Old Navy. But she's always on the prowl for one-of-a-kind clothes and accessories. "I really like little boutiques. I like stuff that I'll wear and people will go, 'Oh, where'd you get that?' They have no idea where I got it. I love that." And Miley is a self-admitted "shopaholic." And her shopping "habit" has gotten worse since she's moved to L.A. "I'm a big shoe person," Miley told *USA Today*. "Sometimes I'll be punky, the next day I'll be preppy."

Even though Lilly and Miley are best buds on screen, in real life, they are complete opposites! Emily's really into soccer. She's been playing since she was six years old. "It's so much fun and my whole family's in on it," Emily told *Popstar!* magazine. "We all go to soccer games." Miley's favorite sport is cheerleading. Growing up, Miley loved to dance, and she thought, what better way to show her moves than by becoming a cheerleader? So that's just what she did when she was a student back in Tennessee. Miley's bubbly personality certainly helps make her a perfect cheerleader. But since Miley's so busy filming and recording these days, she really doesn't have time to be on a team. Although, you can bet that she's always cheering on her costars!

When *Teen* magazine asked Miley and Emily to compare themselves, here's some of what they said: Miley's more outgoing than Emily, although Emily has tons of energy. And Miley's more likely than Emily to ask a guy out on a date. Emily's the bookworm of the duo, and Emily's also the healthier eater. And Miley notes that in real life, the girls' personalities are sort of reversed. On the show, Lilly (Emily) is the crazy one. But according to Miley, Emily's "the one [that] is always like, 'Get this together, Miley. Make sure you read your script tonight. I'll call you on Monday to do this.'"

Miley told *Teen* that when she first saw Emily, she couldn't believe how petite she was. But first impressions aside, Miley and Emily became close friends very fast. Soon they were inseparable on set. Miley explained to *Teen* that, "she and I were really, really close. When we're together we're never quiet because there's so much to talk about and there are so many stories."

As with all friends, Miley and Emily don't agree on

everything. But the two don't ever stay mad at each other for long. Miley told *Discovery Girls* magazine that when she and her friends fight, "I try to be the bigger person. There's no harm in saying 'You know what? Whatever. I'm going to let it roll off.'" Keeping friends is way more important to Miley than being "right" in an argument. And, Miley told *Teen*, "We love each other like sisters. We fight like sisters. It's just like that." The whole *Hannah Montana* cast feels like family to Miley. Miley explained it best to *Teen*: "She's [Emily] kind of like an older sister, so she watches out for me and I do the same for her and make sure she's still having a good time. She's also teaching me how to knit, so she's more of a crafty person and I'm not that good." Emily has gotten Miley into scrapbooking, and even made a cozy blanket for Miley that she sleeps with every night. What a good friend!

On the set, Miley and Emily have a blast acting together, but they also have fun as pranksters. "Emily and I always get into trouble and pull pranks on each other,"

Miley told *J-14* magazine.

Miley is also tight with her other costar, Mitchel Musso. Mitchel plays Oliver, Miley's other best friend. Besides Lilly, Oliver is Miley's only other friend who knows about her dual identities.

Mitchel had a harder time than his costars breaking into the biz. After landing his first commercial gig pretty easily, Mitchel thought showbiz was a breeze. Then came a line of rejections. But Mitchel stuck with it and persevered.

Mitchel had a very small role in the movie *Secondhand Lions*—along with his younger brother, Marc, and Emily Osment's older brother, Haley Joel Osment. And by the time Mitchel auditioned for *Hannah Montana*, he already had a Disney Channel movie under his belt—he starred as Kyle Massey's asthmatic best friend Raymond Figg in *Life Is Ruff*.

But, like his costars, his role on *Hannah Montana* didn't come easily. Of course, he had to audition, and during it, he didn't exactly follow the script. Instead of climbing through a window using a chair to stand on, Mitchel used the desk that the execs, who were auditioning him, were sitting at! That was a pretty bold move, but the improvising helped to land him the part.

Both on and off screen, Miley, Mitchel, and Emily are tight. The threesome can be spotted at the mall together after taping has wrapped for the day, and when they get home, they three-way call one another at night. Miley may have had to uproot herself from Tennessee to move to L.A., but she has certainly found friends who make her feel right at home!

Speaking of friends, what about boys? As in *boyfriends*? Miley has dated a few great guys, but she's not in any hurry to settle down. And she's very picky about who she dates. One thing she can't stand are cocky boys—the ones who are full of 'tude, and of themselves! Miley's skin crawls when she sees dudes who can't take their eyes off themselves in the mirror. Miley also can't figure out the competitive streak that runs through some boys. For them, winning is everything; Miley just wants to have fun.

Miley's ideal date would be a guy who can make her laugh! She likes guys who are funny, silly, and can take her mind off of the pressures of being a star. And of course, she's always on the lookout for a guy who isn't fazed by her fame. And it wouldn't hurt if he was super cute! Miley's sure to find Mr. Right in the end, but in the meantime, she's having lots of fun getting to know all the Mr. Wrongs out there!

Chapter 8

Mom (and Dad) Know Best

Imagine getting the job of a lifetime and then finding out that your dad will be working right alongside you. Talk about cramping your style! But bubbly Miley doesn't mind it at all. "It's kind of cool," she told MediaVillage.com. "But like with anybody, it's kind of weird at the same time. But it's really good to have him there when he can support me. If I ever have a question, my dad's right there!"

Every Monday, at around the same time most kids are getting ready to go to school, Miley crawls out of bed, and gets into the car with her dad. The two have an 8:30 A.M. call time, and Miley has to be on time since she's the star! Father and daughter have a pretty regular morning routine, except for the one time when Billy Ray forgot her! In an interview with *People* magazine, Miley said that one Monday morning she couldn't find her dad. "I'm yelling for my dad up and down the house. So I'm frantic. I go outside, and his car is gone, and my mom's car is gone. So I call my dad and I'm like, 'Dad? Did you forget somebody?' He's like, 'You're not with your mama?'" Of course, Billy Ray sped right home, picked up Miley, and headed straight for the set.

But Miley probably didn't hold her dad's mistake against him. After all, Billy Ray is her loving father, *and* she has to work with him! In an interview with *Discovery Girls* magazine, Miley said this about working with her dad: "It's weird because at home, I'm a normal . . . girl. I'll say, 'Dad, you are so annoying! Leave me alone!'" Miley says that on the long drive from their home to the set, her dad makes her talk about what is bothering her. And Miley has no option but to fess up, since she has a captive audience. It's not like she can get out of the car while they're speeding down the freeway!

But Miley and Billy Ray make sure that they don't

take their work home with them. They don't even practice their lines together at home. "Anything that happens on the set, stays on the set," Miley explained. When they are at home, they act just like a real family, not a made-for-TV family. Miley wants Billy Ray to be her *dad* at home, not her *coworker*.

When Billy Ray was offered the role of Robbie Stewart, he didn't immediately jump at the offer. He was so proud that Miley got the part, and he didn't want to come on the show and mess things up for her. Even though Billy Ray had a pretty successful run with his show *Doc*, he also had his share of letdowns and failures. After all these years, he was still mostly known for "Achy Breaky Heart." All of his follow-up releases up until that point were a disappointment, at least commercially. Perhaps Billy Ray didn't want to carry that stigma with him to Miley's show. However, Billy Ray is now glad he signed on for the show, and he's mighty proud of his little girl, too. "I don't mean to sound like too much of a proud papa," Billy Ray told the

New York Daily News, "but she is just amazing. I've seen that child go to so many auditions and be turned away and just keep on keeping on."

Still, when you are a teenager, there are times when you just don't want your dad around. Since Miley's on the set a lot, and since she's close with her costars, she's probably had some personal conversations with them—you know, the kind of conversations that are definitely *not* for Dad's ears. You could be gossiping with your friends, planning a shopping spree, dishing about your crush, or talking about some hot party. Although Miley says that her dad is "cool," one can't help but think that there are some times when she just wants her space. Luckily, Billy Ray has been careful about giving Miley breathing room. When filming the show, he never gives Miley acting tips. In fact, Miley would be more likely to show her dad what to do!

Even though Billy Ray is not hovering over Miley every second of the day, he can sometimes be pretty embarrassing to have around. One day, one of the prop guys on the set gave Billy Ray a farting machine. Every time Miley walked by, Billy Ray made the machine go off. He did this during the filming of her scenes, too. And, of course, when the fart was heard, Billy Ray would immediately blame Miley as the one who dealt it. How embarrassing! Off the set Dad doesn't let up, either. One time Miley saw Kelly Clarkson at an event, and Billy Ray went right up to her and told her that Miley was her biggest fan. And then he asked Kelly if Miley could take a picture with her. Come on, Dad, give Miley a break!

Miley told MediaVillage.com that her dad can embarrass her during photo shoots, too. "He'll just yell out things I wouldn't want anyone to know. Just random stuff. 'Remember that time when you were a kid?' That kind of stuff." But Dad's antics don't make Miley angry. She knows he's just joking around in order to break the ice. Plus it puts a smile on everyone's face—even Miley's!

Joking aside, Billy Ray can be pretty protective of

his little girl. When Miley first wanted to enter the business, her dad cautioned her against it. He warned her that Hollywood could be a nasty place. And when she was auditioning like crazy, Billy Ray told her to take some time off. He was worried that she was too focused on becoming a star. He wanted her to take time to enjoy the "regular" things in her life, like cheerleading and riding horses. But Miley would hear none of this. She was persistent and pressed on. Her serious attitude certainly impressed her dad. Billy Ray told the *New York Daily News*, "I'm very proud of her that she would set a goal and not stop."

Billy Ray has been a good role model for Miley. "I've never seen him treat anyone less than with respect and love for everyone, down to the fans that wait until three in the morning until his bus pulls out at five," Miley told Oprah. Billy Ray has taught his daughter to never stop chasing her dream. In an interview before the 2006 Country Music Association Awards, Miley was asked what her dad's best advice has been, and Miley said that it was to just be happy and to love what she's doing. But Miley also said that Billy Ray has told her, "No matter what you do, don't listen to me. Listen to your mom!"

Miley's mom, Tish, is her manager, so you can bet that Miley listens to her! Miley says that her mom is stricter than her dad. Billy Ray admits that he's never been good with discipline. What he tries to do, he told *USA Today*, is to "use psychology, make 'em laugh or tell a story to make a point." Tish is the parent that sets the rules for Miley. On a concert night, mom makes sure that Miley's in bed by midnight. And she also makes sure that Miley's up in the morning to study for three hours with her tutor. Tish is fast to set the rules, like the time when Miley refused to change out of a belly shirt and Tish took away her cell phone. "I wasn't very popular for about a week," Tish told *People* magazine. And when Miley lost her credit card, Tish suspended Miley's $300 a month allowance until Miley showed her that she was responsible. Wait a minute—a $300 a month allowance? While that may seem like mega bucks to the average teen, $300 is a drop in the bucket for a girl who's raking in millions of dollars. But putting Miley on a monthly budget really helps to keep her grounded. Punishments can be hard to handle, but Tish told *People* that Miley gets over them pretty quickly. "Most everybody in her life is [telling her] 'yes, yes, yes. You're great.' I'm the one to say, 'You can't do this.' I do this because I love her."

Miley knows that her mom always has her best interest in mind, and mother and daughter find lots of time for fun. "Every day after work my mom and I go shopping," Miley told *USA Today*. And when Billy Ray doesn't want to buy something, Mom's always there with a good reason why it's a must.

Both Tish and Billy Ray work hard at keeping Miley grounded. After all, all that fame *could* go to someone's head—especially a sixteen-year-old! Miley's parents know all too well that a teenage star could get into a lot of trouble. All you have to do is open up any magazine and read about the antics of some of today's stars. "The biggest phenomenon in all this is that the kid's been able to keep her head on her shoulders," Billy Ray told *People* magazine. "She hasn't flipped out. I'm going to knock on wood. I pray every day she can stay on that path."

Besides filming *Hannah Montana* together, Billy Ray and Miley have traveled around the country making appearances and presentations together. At the 2006 World Series in St. Louis, Missouri, Miley and Billy Ray performed the National Anthem together. The pair was scheduled to sing at the game on Wednesday night, but the game was rained out. When they finally did get to sing, Billy Ray was mighty proud. "It's a feeling of going full circle," Billy Ray told OCALA.com. "To look at my little girl standing there, and have the chance to sing together at the World Series is very special. I sing the National Anthem a lot, but I never sang it as a duet with my daughter."

The father-daughter team also presented at the 40th Annual CMA Awards in November 2006. This was the first year that the awards were back in Nashville after a brief run in New York City. Miley must have been excited to be back in her home state! When Miley and Billy Ray hit the podium to present their award, she told him to take off his sunglasses. Billy retorted by saying, "I don't tell you what to wear." Miley's comeback? "That's right. Remember the mullet." Next the two presented at the American Music Awards on November 21, 2006. They also hosted the National Celebration of the Boys & Girls Club, which was held in L.A. on September 16, 2006.

With all those appearances, Billy Ray and Miley sure spend a lot of time together. Billy Ray knows that on top of being Miley's father, he also has to be her friend. Just like the characters they play on TV, Billy Ray lets Miley know that he's always there for whatever she wants to talk about. "Miley and I have a great relationship," Billy Ray said in a Boys & Girls Club interview. "I think it's important as parents and neighbors that we spend quality time with children and to encourage others in our community to do the same."

To that, Miley added, "My dad and I talk all the time about the important stuff in my life. He and my mom know how much I appreciate them, and our relationship is good because we spend time together." And Miley told *People* magazine that she and her dad are "really close. I feel like I can tell my dad anything. When we come home, we forget that we even work together and just hang out."

Miley may be a big star now, but to her parents, she's still their little girl!

Chapter 9

Chart Breaking

Miley loves both her parents, but she's really Daddy's girl. At least, that's whose footsteps she's been following.

In 1992, Billy Ray was at the top of the charts with his hit song, "Achy Breaky Heart." His song spent seventeen weeks at the top of the Billboard 200 chart. His album, *Some Gave All*, sold a whopping 9 million copies, making it a verified chart buster.

But then along came Miley. On October 24, 2006, the *Hannah Montana* CD was released and immediately catapulted to number 1 on the Billboard Top 200 chart. In its first week, the album sold an unbelievable 281,000 copies.

It's true that Miley's amazing voice has contributed to the album's success, but there's something else at work here—Disney. Just like it has done with its TV shows, Disney has done an ingenious job marketing music to kids. In the '90s, Disney sold millions of its sound tracks to movies like *The Lion King* and *The Little Mermaid*. But before, Disney-made stars like Christina Aguilera and Justin Timberlake didn't release their music through Disney.

Today, Disney is singing a different song. The *High School Musical* sound track has sold well over three million copies. *High School Musical* made it to the number 1 spot twice, and was the number one best-selling album of 2006. And the sound track to *The Cheetah Girls 2* debuted in the number 5 slot on the Billboard Top 200 album chart in August of 2006.

Disney has certainly figured out what today's kids want. But what do these new stars have that has made them so successful? Well, first of all, they all have talent. But they are also young, have positive messages in their songs, and a lot of them are girls. In the last few years, magazines like *BOP* and *Tiger Beat* have been plastering female pop stars on their covers. "What these girls are doing is a milestone for pop music," Leesa Coble, editor in chief of *BOP* and *Tiger Beat*, told the *Milwaukee Journal Sentinel*. "In the past it was all about the guys . . . cute boys are still really important, but now you're seeing all these female faces, too." Another thing these new pop stars have going for them is that they get your parents' stamp of approval. No racy lyrics here. Songs from artists like Miley and the Cheetah Girls are good, clean fun. And they are catchy, too!

In the summer of 2006, Miley toured with The Cheetah Girls, performing as their opening act. At each of these shows, on the 40-city tour, you could find thousands of young girls—mostly with their mothers—cheering in the stands. And when Miley—dressed as Hannah Montana—went onstage, the fans went wild! These shows were billed as Cheetah Girls concerts, but Miley's fans were there en masse.

"I'm Hannah Montana! Let's get this party started!

How y'all doing tonight?" is what Miley said when she took the stage at a Cheetah Girls concert. The crowd roared back. They were psyched that Miley/Hannah was the warm-up act for the Girls. When Miley sang, the audience sang along with her—and so did most of the moms!

At each of the Cheetah Girls concerts, Miley could be counted on to belt out her beautiful melodies, with lyrics that really spoke to the audience. When you listen to Miley's lyrics, you feel as though she understands all the stuff you're going through in your life.

In 2006, Miley also appeared on *Good Morning America*, was a presenter at the American Music Awards, performed at the Macy's Thanksgiving Day Parade (on her birthday!), appeared on the CBS special *A Home for the Holidays*, and performed in Walt Disney World's Christmas Day Parade.

When Miley is performing, she feels great. "As soon as I step on that stage, nothing matters. I don't think of it as work. It's just so much fun," she said to *USA Today*.

And it's true: When you watch Miley sing—even when she's dressed like Hannah Montana—it does not look for one minute that she's out onstage because it's a job. This girl truly loves to perform.

But giving a good performance is not as easy as you may think. Sure, Miley has an awesome voice and a personality that wins over any audience, but there's a lot that goes into preparing for a show. Every move that Miley makes on the stage is choreographed. That means hours and hours of working with a choreographer, or dance instructor. Besides working with a choreographer, Miley has to learn all her routines with her backup dancers. All this coordination means lots of rehearsal time. Not only does Miley have to spend time working with the dancers, but she has to go on the road with them, too. Luckily, Miley's sunny personality has enabled her to make fast friends with her crew. And when she steps out onto the stage to sing the songs from her CD, she's super-confident.

The *Hannah Montana* sound track features eight songs performed by Miley (as Hannah), including "The Best of Both Worlds," "Who Said," "Just Like You," "Pumpin' Up the Party," "If We Were a Movie," "I Got Nerve," "The Other Side of Me," and "This Is the Life." Billy Ray gets into the act on "The Other Side of Me," which is actually a duet! Jesse McCartney, Click Five, Everlife, and B5 contributed to the other tracks.

Miley loves to write songs, too. "It's something that comes naturally," she told *Scholastic News*. "It's not a step-by-step thing where I sit down and start writing and singing a tune in my head. Sometimes, I will just hear it and have something stuck with me all day and I will go write about that. Or, maybe I will take something someone said and turn it into a song."

Miley's music has won over her audience by being smart, catchy, and cool. Being cool and family friendly is not easy to pull off, but Miley has certainly done it!

Chapter 10

Here's Miley!

Performing as Hannah Montana is probably pretty cool for Miley Cyrus. But Miley wanted fans to know that she—Miley Cyrus the *real* girl—could sing, too! Miley's wish came true on June 26, 2007, when Walt Disney Records and Hollywood Records released *Hannah Montana 2: Meet Miley Cyrus*. This two-disc CD features ten songs sung by Miley as Hannah Montana, and ten songs sung by Miley as herself.

As soon as the album went on sale, it skyrocketed to number 1 on the Billboard 200, selling at a faster pace than Miley's first CD sold during its debut week. *Hannah Montana 2: Meet Miley Cyrus* stayed in the top 5 for over forty weeks. And when the holidays rolled around, the album jumped back to the top 10 of the Billboard 200 chart. "See You Again" was a breakout single, peaking at number 10 on the Billboard 100. To date, the album has sold more than four million copies worldwide. Talk about a mega success!

Once Miley's second CD was a hit, she could sit back and relax a bit, right? Wrong! On October 18, 2007, in St. Louis, Missouri, Miley kicked off the Best of Both Worlds concert tour. The tour, which was originally scheduled to end on January 9, 2008 in Albany, New York, was extended to January 31, 2008 because it was so popular. Miley traveled to 64 cities on her tour, and played a total of 72 concerts! The Jonas Brothers joined Miley for the first part of the tour, as the opening act. Miley and the super-cute Jonas Brothers played a total of 54 shows together. After the Jonas Brothers decided not to continue on the tour, the mega popular sisters, Aly & AJ, played with Miley from January 11 to January 24. Everlife was the opening act for the last part of the tour, which ended at the American Airlines Arena in Miami, Florida.

Fans all over the country were thrilled to hear the news that Miley was going on tour. They were so thrilled, in fact, that tickets to Miley's concerts sold out practically as fast as the tickets were printed! Controversy swirled around the ticket sales, and some people resold the tickets for thousands of dollars. Fans everywhere begged their parents to stop at nothing to score them tickets to the hottest concert around. And indeed, some did go to extreme lengths: Take the group of fathers, who in a rain-soaked parking lot in St. Louis, strapped on high-heeled stilettos, donned long blond wigs and miniskirts, and raced in the hopes of winning tickets to Miley's show. The men stumbled—and fell—and were probably embarrassed as they dashed to the finish line. But you can bet that the winning dad sure made his daughter happy!

Miley couldn't believe the extremes some fans were going to in order to secure tickets. "It's going to be a good show, but I don't think it's worth what it's going for," she told Ellen DeGeneres. She was bummed that more of her fans couldn't get tickets, which is why she extended her touring schedule. But, she was also excited that the shows sold out!

All controversy aside, Miley had a blast on the Best of Both Worlds tour. She loved performing, night after night, in front of the sold-out crowds. And she also got to hang out with her good friends, the Jonas Brothers. According to *People*, offstage, Miley and the Brothers would battle on the video game *Guitar Hero* and try to out blast each other on their dressing rooms' stereos. "It's your best friends all hanging out together," Kevin Jonas said to *People*. "It's awesome."

Miley had tons of fun on tour, but she also knew she had to give something back. She felt so blessed that she was becoming a huge star and she wanted to help someone else. So Miley donated one dollar from each concert ticket sold to cancer research at City of Hope. Over one million dollars was raised.

Going on a 64-city tour can be grueling. There's

not much time for anything but performing and traveling. (Plus sleeping and eating!) Miley probably had the drill of her tour schedule down pat. But Tish was able to throw Miley a little surprise in the form of a 15th birthday party on November 21, two days before Miley's actual birthday. It was a day off for Miley, and she thought she was going to see one of her favorite bands, Paramore, perform at The Factory in her hometown of Franklin, Tennessee. "I go in and every one of my friends from like second grade was there!" an excited Miley told *People*. Miley's 15th birthday party was a blast! Tish put together a 1980s themed party, and gave Miley an '80s outfit. Two hundred fifty guests, from Miley's pals to stars like Martina McBride, danced the night away!

But the person Miley was most excited to see was her dad. Since Miley travels with her mom when she's on tour, she can go long stretches without seeing Billy Ray. Even though the two iChat and iVideo when Miley's on the road, she really misses her dad a lot. "I look forward to when I go back to [taping] *Hannah Montana* because what I really miss is being with him 24/7." Miley told *People*.

On Miley's actual birthday, November 23, she was in Nashville performing. "I had little surprises throughout my show!" Miley told *People*. During the performance, Miley received fifteen roses from the Jonas Brothers, a cake, and had a big pyrotechnics display. And the best present of all was when Billy Ray joined her onstage to sing their duet "Ready, Set, Don't Go" for the encore. Miley's sister Brandi told *People*, "She [Miley] kept saying she couldn't think of a better way to spend her birthday."

If Miley had one wish to make on her birthday, what would it be? She was a mega star, both as her TV persona Hannah Montana and as the singer Miley Cyrus. What more could a girl want?

Miley
Cyrus

Miley throws up a peace sign in a picture with her fans.

Miley takes the stage to perform for fans.

Miley goes glam with country singer Carrie Underwood.

Miley rocks the 2008 Teen Choice Awards with Fergie.

Miley performs a duet with her dad, Billy Ray Cyrus.

Miley with the Jonas Brothers at Nickelodeon's 2008 Kids' Choice Awards

Miley with *High School Musical* star Vanessa Hudgens

Miley makes an appearance on MTV's *TRL*.

Miley singing

Miley performing in Nashville for *Hannah Montana: The Movie*

Miley and Mickey Mouse at her sweet 16 celebration in Disneyland

Singers Taylor Swift and Katy Perry with Miley at the 2008 MTV Video Music Awards

Miley accepts the 2008 Teen Choice Award for Choice TV Actress: Comedy.

Chapter 10

The Best Movie, Ever!

After a record-breaking, sold-out tour, some people might have wanted to keep all those memories locked in a scrapbook. But not Miley Cyrus. She and her managers decided to make the Best of Both Worlds concert into a movie. Why? "We didn't want people to see only what happens onstage," Miley told *Time For Kids*. "The film goes behind the scenes, so people see the hard work that goes into (doing a tour). They get to see it in the making."

The movie had its Hollywood premiere on January 17, 2008. Miley wore a gorgeous Alberta Ferretti dress, her hair newly darkened. The star-studded crowd included Ashley Tisdale, Vanessa Hudgens, and the Jonas Brothers. When the lights went down in the theater, movie-goers were treated to a special 3-D movie, which gave the effect of actually being at the concert. Both of Miley's worlds—that of Hannah Montana and Miley Cyrus—are featured in the movie.

The film was released on February 1, and was originally scheduled to stay in theaters for just one week. But, just like the live concert, the movie version was a total hit. So Disney decided to extend its run, raking in over $65 million dollars in the process. According to *Vanity Fair* magazine, the movie set several records, including highest-grossing release on a Super Bowl weekend (the movie gave a lot of non-football fans something to do and it earned over $31.1 million that weekend), and the highest per-screen average, making over $45,000 per screen. The movie was later released on DVD.

The stage set itself is something to feast your eyes on: With multilevel platforms, video screens, pyrotechnics, and a ton of dancers, the scene is outrageous. The movie shows Miley rehearsing, performing, and the scene backstage. Rehearsals seem grueling, yet fun. The tour director, Kenny Ortega, admits that it takes a lot of coordinating to get the band, dancers, lights, and pyro all together. In the movie, viewers learn that Miley goes through a lot during each show, and sometimes there are bloopers! One time, Miley was dropped on stage during the song "I Got Nerve." After that she practiced with the dancers some more to make sure that didn't happen again.

With all the songs and scene changes, Miley needs to work fast backstage. Her mom and two other dressers help her with her costume changes, which can be very quick. In the movie, Tish says that for one change, they only have about 37 seconds.

In the concert movie, Miley as Hannah sings "Rock Star," "Life's What You Make it," "Just Like You," "Nobody's Perfect," and "I Got Nerve." When the Jonas Brothers take the stage, she sings "We Got the Party" with them. Miley gets a break when the Jonas Brothers rock out with two songs, "When You Look Me in the Eyes" and "Year 3000."

When the announcer asks the crowd, "Are you ready for Miley Cyrus?" they go wild! Fireworks go off as Miley rises up from the stage. Her brown locks have been curled, and she's wearing jeans, white boots, a white tank, and a leather vest. Chains, necklaces, and a fingerless glove complete her look. Miley wows the crowd with six songs of her own: "Start All Over," "See You Again," "Let's Dance," "Right Here," "I Miss You," and "G.N.O."

In a scene with Billy Ray, he says that he loves the fact that Miley's music is so real. And in a particularly touching moment in the film, Miley says that the song "I Miss You" was written for her grandfather who passed away. Miley admits that fans can relate the lyrics to anything in their lives that they miss, but for Miley, the song is all about her grandfather. During the song, a barefooted Miley sits on the stool playing her guitar and singing while a photo montage of her granddad shows in the background.

And just when the concert-goers think the concert

is over, Miley has one more song in store for them—"Best of Both Worlds." The audience sings along with Miley and a video of Hannah. At the end of the show, Miley looks exhausted, but happy!

Chapter 12

A Peek Backstage

Even though Miley is the star of her TV show, she still has to share a dressing room with her dad! But Miley's not obsessed about her privacy. In fact, it's just the opposite! "My room's like the party room," Miley told *BOP* magazine. "The radio's always on and the music's blasting. No one knocks—they just fling open the door and get ready to party!"

Once, when they were having a party, Emily Osment thought it would be funny if Miley tripped in front of everyone. (Emily's a big practical joker.) So Emily stuck out her foot, and Miley went flying! Was Miley angry? No, she cracked up!

Mitchel Musso loves hanging out in the Cyrus' dressing room, too. Sometimes he'll eat lunch in there, and afterward, Billy Ray gives him guitar lessons.

With the music blasting, Miley is always dancing. It's probably a good way to release some of the tension that has built up over the long day of filming. Miley loves to teach Emily new dances. The two girls pump up the volume and rock out!

If you were to look on the walls of Miley's dressing room, you'd see lots of posters, including one of Kelly Clarkson. Kelly is one of Miley's idols. Some people have told Miley that the two look alike! Miley thinks that Kelly is an amazing singer and performer. In fact, Kelly has inspired Miley to hit the stage. Miley loves Kelly's cool style and would love to have a career as awesome as hers. Besides a poster of her idol, you could see a poster of hottie Orlando Bloom as well as the mega-talented actress Keira Knightley, on her dressing room walls. Miley also likes to clip cool ads from magazines and plaster them on the walls, like one of the hugest diamond rings she ever saw!

Also hanging on a wall of Miley's dressing room is a collage that her best friend Lesley (from Tennessee) made her. It has about forty pictures on it, including shots of the girls wearing cool shades, dressed in their finest, and making silly faces. Also in the collage is a photo of Miley's cheerleading squad. Another collage on a wall has pictures of the Olsen twins, Beyoncé, and Orlando Bloom.

Even though Miley shares her dressing room with her dad, you can tell that she's the decorator. Besides all the posters and collages on the wall, there is other stuff in there that is clearly Miley's, like the pink pillows, the pink candles, the pink picture frames, and a cheetah-print chair that's shaped like a big shoe!

And what are some of Miley's "must haves" in her dressing room? According to *Time For Kids*, Miley must have "Vitamin Water and protein bars that will keep my energy up onstage. And ketchup! Everyone makes fun of me because I eat so much ketchup." Miley puts ketchup on everything! "I put ketchup on pizza, in macaroni, and on the most random things . . . I have to have gobs of it!"

When Miley's on the road, she always rides in style! Miley used to ride around in a tour *van.* Now, she's been upgraded to a tour *bus.* And it's no wonder—when Miley's on the road she needs lots of clothes, both for herself and her alter ego, Hannah. And don't forget the wig!

Miley loves traveling on her tour bus. And who wouldn't when you're riding in style? Miley has her own bunk, complete with a TV. When she needs to chill, she just hops on her bed and pops in a movie. And when she's tired, she cuddles under her Elvis blanket and takes a nap! Miley also never hits the road without her super-cool Sidekick. Come on, how else could she keep in touch with her friends?

Miley's tour bus has sure put on a lot of miles. And her fans are always waiting for her. At Miley's concert debut in Los Angeles, her set opened with the lights down. There was a slow buildup to her entrance—first there was video of her in her dressing room, and then the audience saw footage of her walking toward the stage. The crowd was wild with anticipation. But wait—there was a glitch! The lights suddenly came back on. A stage manager told the audience they were experiencing some technical difficulties. As the minutes ticked by, the audience waited patiently. Then, the whole thing started over again—dressing room and all. But no one seemed to mind.

Miley never lets her fans down. At a record signing in New York City, two thousand fans were lined up, all eager to get her autograph. Some stars have a time limit for their signings. After an hour, they're out of there! But not Miley—she stayed until the last autograph was penned. Miley was probably exhausted after all that signing—not to mention the fact that her hand probably ached—but all she could think about was her fans. She was totally amazed at how patiently they all waited for *her*.

When Miley isn't touring or filming, and has a rare day off, she told *Time For Kids* that she loves playing her guitar and going to the beach. And when she has time for TV, Miley told *Teen* magazine that she loves reality shows. "I always watch *The Real World* and *America's Next Top Model*," Miley admitted. She also confessed that because she was on *That's So Raven* and *Suite Life of Zach & Cody*, she and her little sister became hooked on those shows, too.

When Miley gets back to work and hits the stage, her fans go absolutely wild. "It's totally crazy," Miley told a reporter for Tommy2.net. "After a while you kinda forget. On my first couple concerts, the whole time it kinda threw me off. But they just forget about that because they do a really good job of helping you sing along." During her first couple of shows, Miley got nervous when she grabbed some fans' hands, and they didn't let go. She probably felt as if she was going to go flying into the audience. Not to worry–she stayed onstage.

Miley admits that she sometimes gets nervous before a show. She told *Popstar!* magazine that before her *Radio*

Disney's Totally 10 Birthday Concert, she was excited but definitely had the jitters. Miley had never performed for an audience of that size, so naturally she was feeling the butterflies. She knew that if she could just get through the first song, she'd be fine. And, of course, she was.

With live performances, Miley loves having the energy and excitement of the audience to really pump her up. It is so much fun for her when the audience sings and dances along with her. "I love looking out in the crowd and seeing someone sing along with the lyrics because it helps me not forget the lyrics even if I'm nervous."

See, even stars can catch a case of the nerves.

Chapter 13

Pretty as a Picture?

Miley Cyrus might get nervous at times when she's performing, but she needs to keep a cool head when the paparazzi follow her around, tracking her every move. "Sometimes there'll be like 40 [photographers]," Miley told *Vanity Fair*. "Sometimes twenty, sometimes thirty. Sometimes two. I'll stop and I'll do the picture. It's really funny. They'll buy our dinner and whatever. We've become friends." But with all those photographers around 24/7, Miley must crave some privacy sometimes.

"The good thing about Miley is just last week the paparazzi shot her scarfing down french fries and they had that in every magazine, and she's really great about that," Tish told a reporter from *Vanity Fair*. "She just laughs about it," Tish continued. You have to give Miley a lot of credit for being able to just laugh off what's shown and written about her in newspapers and magazines. That's a really hard thing to do—especially for a teenager, who can be, well, extra sensitive at times!

But it was probably harder for Miley to laugh off the photos of her that circulated on the Internet in April 2008. In the photos, Miley's belly is showing and part of her bra can be seen. For most people, such photos would be seen as no big deal. But for a teen that is constantly in the public eye, and is viewed as a role model, the photos caused quite a controversy. "The pictures of me on the Internet were silly, inappropriate shots," Miley told *People* magazine. "I appreciate all the support of my fans, and hope they understand that along the way I am going to make mistakes and I am not perfect. I never intended for any of this to happen and I am truly sorry if I have disappointed anyone." Miley continued by saying, "Most of all, I have let myself down. I will learn from my mistakes and trust my support team. My family and my faith will guide me though my life's journey." Miley learned an important lesson from all of that, though. She knows now to be very careful when any camera is around—even if it belongs to someone she thinks is a friend—and to be very careful who she sends pictures to!

On the heels of the Internet photos came a photo spread in *Vanity Fair*, shot by renowned photographer Annie Leibovitz. In one of the most controversial photos of the shoot, Miley is wrapped in a bed sheet, looking over her shoulder, with her back exposed. When the photos were first taken, Miley was pleased with the outcome. "I think it's really artsy," Miley told a reporter from *Vanity Fair*. "It wasn't in a skanky way . . . And you can't say no to Annie. She's so cute. She gets this puppy-dog look and you're like, okay." But Miley never could have imagined the reaction the photos would get!

When the photos came out in the magazine, a lot of people were shocked. They felt that it was inappropriate for Miley to be photographed in that way. The Disney

Channel, too, was critical of the photos. "Unfortunately . . . a situation was created to deliberately manipulate a 15-year-old in order to sell magazines," a network statement said. Miley's family, friends, and publicist were all quick to support Miley in the media, blaming the picture on the photographer.

But Annie Leibovitz defended her art. In a statement released by *Vanity Fair*, Leibovitz said, "I'm sorry that my portrait of Miley has been misinterpreted. Miley and I looked at fashion photographs together and we discussed the picture in that context before we shot it. The photograph is a simple, classic portrait, shot with very little makeup, and I think it is very beautiful." And *Vanity Fair* stated, "Miley's parents and/or minders were on the set all day. Since the photo was taken digitally, they saw it on the shoot and everyone thought it was a beautiful and natural portrait of Miley."

And what did Miley think about all this? In a statement released through her publicist, Miley said,

"I took part in a photo shoot that was supposed to be 'artistic' and now, seeing the photographs and reading the story, I feel so embarrassed. I never intended for any of this to happen and I apologize to my fans who I care so deeply about." In an interview with *Seventeen* magazine, Miley said this about her experience with the pictures: "I learned that I'm stronger than I perceived myself to be. And I really feel grateful to my fans for everything they've done for me, and for standing by me. I really do want what's best for *them*." Miley really was horrified by the fan response to the pictures, and she really regrets having them taken. She made a mistake, but she's learned from it. And now she knows what *not* to do at her next artsy photo shoot!

Chapter 14

Breaking Out

On July 22, 2008, Miley Cyrus came out with her second album, *Breakout*. You're probably thinking that it was her *third* album, but *Breakout* is Miley's second album as *Miley*. And with this album, Miley really made her mark as a pop star sensation!

The title of the album is very significant—Miley was "breaking out" on her own. With *Breakout*, she was shedding her image of Hannah Montana. Sure, she did that a bit with The Best of Both Worlds tour, but *Breakout* was hers alone. Miley told a reporter from *Time For Kids* that *Breakout* is different from her other albums because "it's a little more personal. You get to know more about different things that have gone on in my life."

Miley cowrote eight of the twelve songs on the

album. "Right now my age group is between four and twenty," Miley told *Entertainment Tonight*. With the album, Miley is trying to "embrace the older audience a little more. Miley told *MTV News* that the album is "for every teenager, or any woman in general. Most of my songs are for the girls who hate their current or ex-boyfriends."

That statement rings especially true for "7 Things," which was the first single from the album to be released onto the airwaves back in May. And on July 18, four days before the album's release, Miley showcased the song on *Good Morning America's Summer Concert Series*. Miley played to a packed crowd at Bryant Park. She took to the stage wearing shorts, heeled boots, and a long-sleeved plaid shirt. She looked absolutely thrilled to be giving the crowd a sneak peak of her song. But Miley didn't let the screaming crowd get to her head—she even confessed to one of the hosts of the show that she was afraid that no one would show up for the concert!

The song "7 Things," a tune in which Miley sings

about seven things that a girl hates and the seven that she loves about her boyfriend, debuted at 84 on the Billboard Hot 100 chart and within two weeks it rose to number 10. The song peaked at number 9, making it Miley's biggest hit.

The song was really the breakout hit on Miley's album. It received lots of airplay, and girls all over the country were memorizing the lyrics. In an interview with *Entertainment Tonight*, Miley played a little game of "name 7 things":

Miley's 7 Favorite Cities: Chicago, Detroit, Nashville, St. Louis, Miami, New York/New Jersey (she counted this as one!), Kentucky.

7 Words to Describe Miley: adventurous, positive, courageous, loving, giggly, hyper, heart for God.

7 Things Miley Wants to Do Before Her Life is Over: swim in the Red Sea, fly in a helicopter, see the Great Wall of China, go to Australia and see a toilet flush the other way, write a book, meet Chris Martin from Coldplay, and make *Breakout* hit number 1 on the Billboard charts.

Well, making *Breakout* number 1 was sure easy! On the first day the album was released, it sold 110,000 copies. It debuted at number 1 on the Billboard 200 chart. In the first week alone, the album sold over 370,000 copies! To date, the album has sold over one million copies.

Lots of teens and tweens can relate to the lyrics of the songs on *Breakout*. A lot of the songs deal with relationships—meeting someone and breaking up. "I hope [fans] can just take away a lot from what I've learned," Miley told *MTV News*. "Like it says, it's a 'breakout' record. It kind of explains what I've been going through, so it's kind of a love song/breakup record," Cyrus explained. Miley continued by saying, ". . . you have to believe me that it's going to turn out great." And what is Miley's favorite song on the album? "Bottom of the Ocean," she tells *Time for*

Kids, "because it has more emotion than any other song. Even though all the songs on the CD are really heartfelt, I feel like it has more of what I want to say."

Two of the songs on the album that Miley didn't write are covers. "These Four Walls" was originally recorded by Cheyenne Kimball. And "Girls Just Wanna Have Fun" was originally recorded by the funky Cyndi Lauper.

But with the songs she does write, Miley told a reporter from *Time For Kids* that she gets her ideas for the lyrics from kids. "When I'm out doing a concert and I look into the audience, and see kids singing and dancing, it really inspires me."

Keep on writing those songs, Miley!

Chapter 15

Crushed

When you're a gorgeous star like Miley Cyrus, there are always rumors flying around about who you're crushing on and who you're dating. Miley probably can't step out on the street with a guy without having her picture snapped, and a story run the next day about her and her new beau.

For a while there were rumors circulating that Miley and Nick Jonas were an item. Miley verified this eventually, but only after the pair broke up. "We became boyfriend and girlfriend the day we met," Miley confessed to *Seventeen* magazine. Apparently Nick was on a mission to meet Miley, and told her that he thought she was so beautiful and that he really liked her. This must have set Miley's heart on fire, because she liked him, too! "Nick and I loved each other. We *still* do, but we were *in love* with each other," Miley said. Miley continued by saying that the pair was together for two years.

It was very hard for Miley to keep her relationship a secret. And what made it especially difficult was the fact that they were arguing a lot. Since Miley and Nick were both working so much, they didn't get to spend as much time together as they wanted. Plus, with all the long hours they were both putting in, they were tired. And when someone's tired, they can get cranky! ". . . it was just like, 'When am I going to get some time with my boyfriend?'" Miley told *Seventeen.*

Miley and Nick broke up right before they went on stage during her Best of Both Worlds concert tour. In an interview with *Seventeen*, Miley said that she asked Nick, "Is this just too much for us right now? Is this something that is really inconvenient at this time in your life?" Nick told her that this *was* a really hard time for him, and that he thought they needed a break. With that, the two started to cry. Talk about heartbreak!

For months after the breakup, Miley was really sad. She admitted to *Seventeen* that she cried for about a month straight! In her despair, she dyed her hair black. When they were dating, Nick wanted her to get highlights, which she did. But after Nick, Miley wanted something different. ". . . on the day we broke up, I was like, I want to make my hair black now—I don't want to look pretty; I want to look *hard-core*." Eventually, Miley went back to her lighter hair after some of the pain of the breakup had passed.

It's hard when you break up with someone you love, and a lot of times you want to do something drastic to rebel to make yourself feel better. Miley is someone who has a good head on her shoulders, so the worst thing she did was dye her hair. For her, dying her hair showed the world that she was someone different without Nick. Although breaking up with someone is really hard, and you feel like you'll never get over it, you do! That was true for Miley, too. "The Nick thing is in the past, and I can't be living there. But I feel great."

Even though Miley and Nick aren't an item anymore, they're still friends. It's hard to be friends with someone you once dated, but Miley is one tough cookie, and she was able to go forward with a friendship. After all, the two do work together now and then! "We're very close, but definitely in a different way," Miley told *Seventeen*.

Before Miley dated Nick Jonas, she told *J-14* that she and Dylan Sprouse (of the *Suite Life of Zack & Cody* fame) "dated for a day." But the two are really just friends. When they were spotted at a movie theater together, along with some of Dylan's friends, Dylan said, "We were just going to the movies and decided to invite some friends, including Miley. We had a jolly good time."

Rumors were also flying that Miley was dating model and aspiring country singer, Justin Gaston. Justin is five years older than Miley and a certified hottie. Miley would neither confirm nor deny the rumors that the two are an item. But Justin was seen attending church with the Cyrus clan, at Disney's Concert of Hope, at Miley's sweet sixteen birthday party at Disneyland, and more.

Boyfriend or not, Billy Ray likes Justin. Billy Ray told *Access Hollywood*, "He [Justin] actually reminds me a lot of myself when I was a 20-year-old and I was living and searching for the dream. He's got a great heart and soul, and a lot of determination. I think the true measure of a man is when you measure his heart." So, if Miley and Justin are an item, they have Dad's stamp of approval!

Miley loves being in a relationship, and she certainly has her pick of super cute guys, but she's also very okay with being single. She loves getting the chance to focus on herself and what makes her happy, and getting to spend lots of quality time with her friends. She knows it will probably be a long time before she's ready to settle down with one guy, so for now, she's just having fun!

Chapter 16

A Banner Year

Miley Cyrus must have known she was going to have a great 2008 from the moment the calendar flipped from December 31, 2007 to January 1, 2008. Miley kicked off the new year with an appearance on *Dick Clark's New Year's Rockin' Eve.* This classic television show has aired every New Year's Eve since 1972. Since 2005, Ryan Seacrest has been hosting the portion of the show that is filmed in Times Square. Thousands of people crowd the New York City streets, watching performers and waiting for the famed "ball" to drop, signifying the start of the new year. At the 2008 show (which really started in 2007!), Miley sang "Start All Over" and "G.N.O." Later on in the show she performed "We Got the Party" with the Jonas Brothers.

The year only got better and better from there! With a hit movie and a record-breaking CD under her belt, what more could she want? Well, a star like Miley needs to shine, and shine she did. You could hardly open a magazine or flip a channel on your TV without seeing Miley's smiling face. In fact, in 2008, *Time* magazine listed Miley among artists and entertainers as one of the "100 Most Influential People."

Miley did her rounds of talk shows and teen magazine interviews. But probably one of her most exciting interviews was with Barbara Walters. "The Barbara Walters Special" aired right before the Academy Awards show, and was watched by millions. Barbara also interviewed superstar Harrison Ford, Academy Award nominee Ellen Page (of *Juno* fame), and Emmy Award nominee Vanessa Williams (she plays Wilhelmina on *Ugly Betty*) that night, so Miley was in good company.

Barbara Walters has the knack for getting her guests to open up, and Miley was no exception. Miley told

Barbara about her acting aspirations, being a role model, and staying grounded. When Barbara asked Miley about the public pressure to be perfect, Miley commented, "I've been put in the position where, you know, there's cameras around all the time and . . . it's like you can't escape, you know, the press. And you can't escape the world that you live in. It's hard because I'm young, you know, to be out with my friends and just be like, 'Oh, you know, there's someone snapping pictures.'" It was clear from Miley's comment to Barbara Walters that having cameras on her 24/7 is really hard!

Miley and Barbara talked about how there are lots of young Hollywood stars who let the fame get to their heads, and then get into trouble themselves. But Miley said that she doesn't really rebel, and she relies on her family to keep her focused. "I know that some people don't have a family to fall back on like I have," Miley said. "I think that a lot of these people . . . do have Christian families and they're just not seeing that they're so much greater than the materialistic things that are there right now like going out [to] parties."

Barbara also talked to Miley's mom, who admitted, "I wouldn't say I'm like really, really strict. But I definitely have a lot of boundaries." Tish proudly told Barbara that she always knew Miley would be a star. "From the time she was two [or] three years old, she would stand at Billy Ray's dad's house on the stairs and sing 'Tomorrow' at the top of her lungs."

Right after people watched Barbara Walter's special, they could keep their TVs tuned into the Academy Awards show. Glammed-out stars walked the red carpet, stopping for photo ops and interviews. But one of the most glamorous of all was Miley Cyrus. With her hair parted on the side and pulled back into a low ponytail, and wearing an elegant red Valentino dress, Miley looked superb! When Ryan Seacrest nabbed Miley for a short interview on the carpet, Miley admitted that she hoped that one day she'd be at the Oscars for a movie that she had starred in! And when she took to the stage at the ceremony, Miley introduced Kristin Chenoweth singing "That's How You Know" from the movie *Enchanted*.

Miley might have just been a presenter at the Oscars, but she was a *host* at another prestigious awards show—the *Teen Choice Awards*. The show was on August 4 at Universal City's Gibson Amphitheatre. For Miley's opening number, she performed her hit single "7 Things." As Miley sang, she ran in every direction, stopping only to deliver a rose to audience member Fergie. And Fergie was absolutely starstruck when she got the gift from Miley. Acting like any other Miley Cyrus fan, Fergie jumped up and down!

And just like Fergie, Miley had her own reasons to celebrate that night, too. Besides the great thrill of hosting the show, Miley walked away with three awards for choice TV comedy (for *Hannah Montana*), comic actress, and female artist. What a night!

But the *Teen Choice Awards* was Miley's first

hosting job of the year. On April 14, she co-hosted the 7th Annual CMT Music Awards with her dad, Billy Ray. The awards ceremony took place at the Curb Event Center at Belmont University in Nashville, Tennessee. Even though Miley was battling a throat infection that night (some reports say she had a 103-degree temperature the night before!) she looked beautiful on the red carpet, wearing a backless, halter-style, floor-length white gown with red flowers. And Miley must have been feeling pretty great when she took to the stage with her dad to sing "Ready, Set, Don't Go."

However, Miley's year wasn't just filled with fame and fortune. Miley knows how lucky and blessed she is, so she wanted to give something back. Uniting with fifteen of the hottest female singers in the world, including Mariah Carey, Beyoncé, Rihanna, Fergie, and Carrie Underwood, Miley took part in an hour-long fundraiser for cancer research. The women sang the beautiful song "Just Stand Up," which was released as a single, and has been given lots of airplay as a video.

Miley also took part in the "Concert for Hope," a special event benefiting cancer research and treatment programs at City of Hope. "I just think it's really important," Miley told a reporter from the *Times Online* (UK) about her support for City of Hope. "Just because so many kids have all these dreams . . . the people that get diagnosed with these type of cancers and stuff at such a young age, they never feel like they have an opportunity to really dream." Miley told the reporter that she wants to raise money to help find a cancer cure "to give these kids an opportunity to live their dreams. 'Cause the future is all about the young ones now."

Hosted by Almost Amy, the recording group featuring Mark Ballas and Derek Hough from *Dancing with the Stars*, the City of Hope concert raised $1.2 million. The concert featured Miley Cyrus, the Jonas Brothers, and Demi Lovato, who played to a sold-out crowd at Gibson Amphitheater in Los Angeles.

At the concert, Miley took to the stage after the Jonas Brothers. She wore a pair of tight jeans, and a T-shirt featuring an image of her older brother Trace's band, Metro Station. Miley had five musicians, two backup vocalists, and eight dancers with her as she burned up the stage singing songs form her *Breakout* album. "We are grateful to Miley Cyrus, the Jonas Brothers, Demi Lovato, and their fans for their support of City of Hope and our lifesaving mission," Dr. Michael A. Friedman, president and chief executive officer of City of Hope, said on the foundation's website. "Their extraordinary efforts will ensure medical advances continue and that we quickly bring new treatments to patients who need them." Miley's charitable commitments are indeed extraordinary!

On October 12, Miley rocked out in London when she played at *BBC Switch Live*. This massive concert, suitable for the underage set, was all the rage in England. Miley took to the stage at the Hammersmith Apollo and the crowd went wild! Miley played with a lineup that included Fall Out Boy and Ne-Yo.

Then, in November, Miley hit the big screen again. Well, her face didn't exactly light up the screen, but her voice did. Miley voiced Penny in *Bolt*, Disney's 47th animated feature. The movie is the story of a dog named Bolt (voiced by John Travolta) who has lived his entire life on the set of a TV show in which he plays a superhero dog. Bolt thinks that his superpowers are real on and offstage! Miley plays Penny, Bolt's on-screen owner. When Bolt is accidentally shipped from his Hollywood soundstage to New York City, he realizes that he must rely on something other that his "superpowers" to get himself home to Penny.

During the holiday season, Miley was featured on the Disney album *All Wrapped Up*. On the album, she sings her own version of "Santa Claus is Coming to Town" and it rocks! Also featured on this special album are the Jonas Brothers, Jordan Pruitt, and Demi Lovato.

In addition to all the talk shows, award shows, and

special concerts, a special honor was bestowed upon Miley when Madame Tussauds in New York City unveiled a wax figure of Miley in March. Madame Tussauds is a wax museum that originated in London, England. The museum was set up by Marie Tussaud, who was a wax sculptor. Tussaud was born in 1761 in France, and later moved to London, where she set up a wax museum. The museum has become a major tourist attraction, and has branches in several cities around the world. Wax figures in the museum include sports stars, musicians, actors, and politicians. Miley's figure is wearing skinny black jeans, a blue and gold silk top, and open-toe red shoes. And of course, she is smiling!

Yes, Miley certainly had a lot to smile about in 2008!

Chapter 17

The Most Important Role

If you're a star with a hit TV show, a groundbreaking movie, three chart-busting CDs, and sold-out concerts across the country, you're probably going to find your face plastered over every teen mag. So it's no wonder that girls everywhere are going to look up to you. They will follow your every move, track what you wear, know where and what you eat, and who you hang with. Basically, they are going to know everything about you.

There's lots of pressure put on teenage stars. You have to literally watch your every step. As a teen star, you wouldn't want to do anything that could be construed as being "over the edge." Essentially, you need to walk the straight and narrow.

But people have been obsessed with stars since

the beginning of time, right? Ask your parents and grandparents about Elvis (who made teenage girls faint) or the Beatles (who made girls cry), or David Cassidy (who plastered many a wall). What's different about star obsession today?

Today, teens can worship their stars 24/7—you can watch them on TV, you can download their tunes onto your iPod, and you can get fan club alerts blasted to your e-mail inbox and your cell phone. Today's teens feel closer to their favorite celeb than ever before. Some have even come to think of their star as their close personal friend.

Chances are that Miley's not your bud, but she is the kind of girl you'd want to befriend—and the kind of girl you can look up to as well. When a reporter from *Time For Kids* asked Miley if it makes her nervous to know that she's a role model for so many fans, here's how Miley answered: "It does. It adds pressure, but it also makes me super excited to know that people are looking up to me." What, according to Miley, makes a good role model?

"I think just knowing who you are before you try to help people find themselves. I think you have to know who you are."

Miley is totally aware of all the social pressures that have been put on her. As the middle child in her family, she's always been looked up to by her younger siblings. The younger family members have always asked Miley for advice, which she is ready and willing to dole out. Miley is a great role model for her siblings—they can see that her success has certainly not gone to her head. She is still the honest, down-to-earth sister they know and love. Miley can feel confident that her parents have raised her well and have taught her how to be a good person.

Billy Ray knows all too well the pressures that come with the biz. And he has cautioned Miley to watch out for the good as well as the bad. Billy Ray is also confident that Miley won't be a wild teenager who is always getting into trouble. "I see her being Miley Cyrus," he told *USA Today*. "She will never be somebody else. She's got her own thing. I think she takes and borrows and hints at a little bit of a lot of people . . . but she's her own person."

Miley knows that Billy Ray has been a good role model for her. And neither of her parents gives her the star treatment at home, which keeps her grounded. Like any other kid, Miley still has to make her bed and clean her room!

Miley has learned from her dad to treat her fans with respect. On more than one occasion when growing up, Miley saw her dad get hounded by fans during family time, yet Billy Ray always made time for them. He would tell Miley, "These people are supporting you. Be good to them." Dad has certainly taught Miley well.

On July 13, 2004, Miley was attending a fan club event for Billy Ray that was held during the CMA Music Festival in Nashville. In the middle of the event, Billy Ray and Tish surprised their daughter with a Daisy Rock Girl Guitar. What was so special about that? Well, it just so happens that the Daisy Rock Company was making Miley their youngest endorsee ever.

The mission of Daisy Rock, which is the only guitar company to manufacture guitars specifically for girls, is to empower young girls to play music and reach their goals. Miley's drive and ambition certainly fit the bill. "When my wife, Tish, and I learned about Daisy Rock Guitars for Girls, we knew this was the perfect guitar and attitude for Miley," Billy Ray said.

And if you look at a Daisy Rock Girl guitar, you'll notice that they're bright and sparkly—just like Miley!

Chapter 18

The Sweetest Sweet Sixteen

Lots of girls can't wait to turn sixteen. Some see this age as a step closer to being able to drive. Other see this age as a step closer to becoming independent from their parents. Others see this age as a chance to PARTY! For many girls, turning sixteen is a reason to have a sweet sixteen party. Some such parties are strictly family affairs or include a few close friends. Other parties are huge blowouts, such as those featured on the MTV reality series *My Super Sweet Sixteen.*

Miley's sweet sixteen was indeed a blowout, although without the drama that's featured on the reality show! For Miley's sweet sixteen, she celebrated at the happiest place on earth—Disneyland! Miley's family closed down the entire park for the occasion, allowing 5,000 of her fans and friends to attend. Fans paid $250 each for the privilege of partying with the almost 16-year-old. (Miley's bash was on October 5; her actual birthday wasn't until November 23).

Proceeds from the event went to Youth Service America, which according to the group's website, "is a resource center that partners with thousands of organizations committed to increasing the quality and quantity of volunteer opportunities for young people, ages 5–25, to serve locally, nationally, and globally." At the party, Miley honored some of Youth Service America's volunteers. She also presented the group with a check for $1 million from Disneyland Parks and Resorts. "The best part of the party is we're going to recognize some really cool kids from Youth Service America who are giving back to their community. That's so awesome because I think it's really important for kids like us to volunteer," Miley was quoted as saying on YSA's website.

The party itself was incredible. There was a

parade of stars, and even a purple carpet since purple is Miley's favorite color! Throughout the evening, some of the park's attractions, such as Space Mountain, Big Thunder Mountain, and Pirates of the Caribbean remained open for the partygoers to enjoy. Other activities included receiving a "Hannah Montana makeover" and playing the Disney Interactive Studios rhythm video game "Ultimate Band."

Disneyland took the opportunity that night to promote their upcoming "What Will You Celebrate?" theme. The park encourages tourists to take "celebration vacations" with their families. Starting in 2009, Disneyland and Walt Disney World guests are able to gain free admission on their birthday with valid ID and proof of date of birth.

Besides the paying fans, the park was crawling with celebrities that night. Big names such as David Archuleta, Demi Lovato, Julianne Hough, Jennie Garth, Steve Carell, Cindy Crawford, Tyra Banks, and Jennifer Love Hewitt were all in attendance. Miley told *Entertainment Tonight* that the party was the "most amazing, magical night I could have asked for."

But the biggest draw of the night was Miley's birthday concert. Billy Ray opened up for his daughter with a few of his songs, which of course included "Achy Breaky Heart." Miley's "boyfriend" Justin Gaston even took to the stage to sing. And when Miley took the stage, she wore a white ruffled skirt and a white vest with "Sweet 16" printed on the back. The birthday girl sang four songs, including "Breakout" and "G.N.O."

Miley was asked by several interviewers what she wanted for her birthday, and she always answered with "a car." But Miley did reveal one gift she got—an adorable little puppy named Sophie. Although Miley probably had a huge birthday wish list, she was grateful for the fabulous party given by her parents. "My parents shut down Disneyland, so I'm good for a while," the Associated Press reported Miley as saying. Tish and Billy Ray were probably only too happy to throw the sweet sixteen party for their girl. As Billy Ray told *Access Hollywood*, the party was "just a celebration of life; that's what tonight is."

When it came time to sing happy birthday, Miley was joined on stage by her family and—guess who?—Mickey Mouse. Her cake featured sixteen giant inflatable candles. There was also a specially designed fireworks display over Sleeping Beauty's Castle to top off the night. The celebration lasted until 11:00 P.M., but Miley's memories of that night will probably last forever!

Chapter 19

Styling!

No matter if it's preppy, goth, sporty, glam, or funky, everyone has her own style. In Miley's case, however, she needs to have three fashion IDs—as Miley Stewart, as Hannah Montana, and as Miley Cyrus. How is she able to keep them straight? It's simple—she's a pro!

But Miley knows that she has to be mindful of what she wears, since her young fans look up to her. True she has a stylist, but Miley told Oprah Winfrey, "I say what I'm comfortable in and what I like and nothing that's too out there. I like to look kind of like what girls would want to look up to, and their moms and dads will say, 'Hey, that's cool. That's different.'" Miley continued to comment on her style, saying, "I look way young and that's . . . more comfortable for me."

As Hannah Montana, plain is definitely not the name of the game. Hannah loves bling and everything that sparkles. From her dazzling clothes to her sparkly makeup, Hannah really shines. Wanna dress like Hannah? Here's a shopping list:

- **Hair**: Blond wig (the wig that Miley wears as Hannah is *really* heavy—in fact, there are times onstage when Miley is afraid it will fall off!)
- **Shirts**: A long, flowing, antique-inspired blouse; a sheer top with a camisole underneath; a studded tank top
- **Dresses**: Definitely mini!
- **Jackets**: Anything cropped; anything with rhinestones; a distressed-denim jacket
- **Shoes**: Cowboy boots; suede boots; leather boots
- **Pants**: Leggings; skinny jeans
- **Accessories**: A colorful glittery scarf; a

beaded necklace; long chain necklaces; dangly earrings; chunky bangle bracelets

Miley told *People* magazine that she and her character Hannah Montana both like to constantly change up their style. "That's how I think my real personality shines through. I change it so much," Miley admitted. But even though the two like to change their styles, Miley thinks that Hannah is much more girly than she is in real life. And although Miley gets dressed up for photo shoots, she says "in real life, if I'm wearing a dress, I'm wearing Chuck Taylors with it. I've never been super girlie."

Even though the off-screen Miley readily confesses that she's a shopaholic—she loves shopping for shoes and bags—she has a really down-to-earth style. On her tour bus, Miley can be found wearing sweats, a hooded tee, and Uggs. And on a photo shoot for *Popstar!* magazine, Miley showed up wearing Victoria Secret sweats from their Pink line with a hoodie. "I don't always go for clothes that are the most expensive," she told *Teen* magazine.

"It doesn't matter how little something costs. I [recently] got six-dollar shoes, and I was like, 'Yeah.'" In fact, Miley counts Target as one of her fave stores! Miley loves Target because she can get clothing that's not too expensive, yet it's trendy. That way, you don't feel like you've wasted your money if what you've bought goes out of style in two weeks!

Miley is always willing to take risks when it comes to fashion. She's not one to follow the latest fashion trend. Instead, she likes to be a trendsetter. Sometimes, at first glance, Miley picks out a top and pants that she thinks look really bad together. But once she puts them on and accessorizes, they look great! Miley's always telling people to do their own thing when it comes to fashion. Who knows—you may be starting a fashion trend of your own!

But, like lots of teens, Miley isn't always confident about her looks. She spends many hours in front of the mirror—and she doesn't always like what she sees! She complains about her hair, her nose, and her teeth. But then she snaps out of it, her self-confidence shines through, and she tells herself that she's beautiful.

In an interview with *Girls' Life* magazine, Miley let loose a little secret: She hates getting dressed up. If you were to see her at red-carpet events, she'd probably be holding her shoes. After all, stilettos can be hard on a girl's feet! "If I could go to premieres in my sweats, I would! If you wear baggy things and just put a little T-shirt with it, you'll look cute. A girl's outfit doesn't have to be, you know, everything all out there."

Like her alter ego, Miley likes wearing jewelry. She likes necklaces and earrings, but she adores bracelets. She wears a charm bracelet that her mom made for her, as well as two bracelets that fans made for her. And she never takes them off. In some photos of Miley, you won't see her bracelets, but that's because they've been airbrushed out (a little trick that the fashion industry uses when they don't want you to see something!). One of Miley's bracelets is a plastic band, like the kind you get at a water park. When she first had it, it was orange. Now it looks like a strand of gray string. Her mom thinks it's pretty nasty, but Miley refuses to take it off. Miley also has a bracelet that says "live and love" that she got from a friend. But the piece of jewelry that is the most special to Miley is a ring. In some photos, you can see her wearing it on her right ring finger. The ring, which basically looks like a plain band, was originally two rings that her dad gave her mom. As a gift for one Valentine's Day, Billy Ray had the rings made into one and gave it to Tish. Tish then gave it to Miley. How sweet!

Compared to Hannah, Miley told *People* magazine, "Her style is more typical-girlie, and I'm very much a tomboy. That's what I get in trouble for a lot. Mom is like, 'It's not going to hurt you to be a girl one day.'"

When it comes down to it, the fashion style of the real-life Miley Cyrus and TV's Miley Stewart is pretty similar. Sure, Miley has to get dressed up when she goes out in public, or at photo shoots, but when she's off the set, casual clothes are just fine. Miley told *People*. But like Hannah, Miley is always changing up her style. " . . . I change it up so much," Miley admitted in a *People* interview. "My grandma and my mom have used the same makeup their whole lives. I'll never be able to do that. My favorite thing one day will be my least favorite thing the next because I find things that I like much better."

But if you were to go shopping with Miley, here's a possible shopping list:

- **Shirts**: Cotton tanks; short- and long-sleeved tees; graphic tees; tunics; camis; hoodies; a white, lacy, button-down blouse
- **Dresses**: A slip dress; a flowing mini-dress to go over leggings; sparkly mini-dress; long gowns (but only for special occasions!)
- **Skirts**: Jean miniskirt; flouncy miniskirt
- **Jackets**: Sweatshirts; a cropped, knit sweater; a denim jacket; a basic black blazer; a white sleeveless vest

- **Shoes:** Canvas sneakers; leather boots with heels; chunky leather boots; dressy sandals; flip-flops
- **Socks:** Long tube socks
- **Pants:** Skinny jeans; basic jeans; jean shorts; army camouflage pants; drawstring pants; sweats; leggings
- **Hats:** Knit caps; baseball caps
- **Accessories:** Lots of bracelets; simple chokers; a western leather tote

Although Miley likes to shop in stores like Target, Forever 21, Wet Seal, and Urban Outfitters, she does put on the designer labels when she's headed out somewhere special. Here are some places where Miley's been spotted all dressed up:

- On the *American Idol* special "Idol Gives Back," Miley wore J Brand 910 jeans paired with a sequined cami.

- At Nickelodeon's *Kids' Choice Awards 2008*, Miley stepped out in a Stella McCartney rhinestone-studded tank dress and carried a ruby Swarovski clutch.
- At the Grammy Awards on February 10, 2008, Miley sported a fabulous Celine dress.
- At the 80th Annual Academy Awards, Miley graced the red carpet in a floor-length, red Valentino gown.

When going out, putting on a cool outfit is not enough for most girls, and Miley is no exception—makeup is a must! While Miley doesn't wear a ton of makeup, she's usually seen with black eyeliner and black mascara. Her lipstick isn't too flashy—she either wears clear lip gloss or something in the light pink family. On her eyes, Miley tries different shadows—from a pink and gray combo, to dark purple, to lime green, to bronze or silver. But even when the makeup comes off, Miley's still beautiful!

As for hair, Jennifer Llewelyn, Miley's hair stylist on

her Best of Both Worlds tour, did Miley's hair in two basic ways—curly and straight. Even Miley's hair got the best of both worlds! To get Miley's look, first take some large hair clips and separate the top and bottom layers of your hair. Blow-dry the bottom half of your hair first, then move on to the top. Use a round brush when blowing the top of your hair to add some volume. Be sure to apply a heat-protection product to your hair so it won't frizz out! To get Miley's straight look, you'll need a flat iron. Remember to iron your hair in sections, and be careful—a flat iron can get *very* hot! If you want Miley's curly look, use a curling iron. Again, be careful when using this tool. Change up the direction of the curls to get a naturally curly look.

While most teens like Miley know that they have to eat well in order to be healthy, Miley likes to dive into junk food every now and then. But, hey, who doesn't? Some of her favorite foods—if you can really call them food—are gummy bears and cookie dough. Her mom doesn't really think Miley should eat cookie dough, since it contains raw eggs—which could make you sick—but Miley tells her mom not to worry. A typical teenager's response! And when it comes to the catering that's frequently offered to Miley on a photo shoot, she'd much rather have a fast-food meal. And of course, Miley loves to put ketchup on everything.

No matter what she eats, no matter what she wears, the verdict is in: Fans love Miley inside and out!

Chapter 20

She's Got Music

Miley likes to constantly vary her fashion style, but that's not the only thing she likes to change up: In many interviews, Miley has admitted that her favorite music is eclectic, too. From country, to pop rock, to pop punk, to R&B, Miley's taste covers a wide range. Here are some of the artists who inspire Miley:

Fellow Tennessean, Dolly Parton, is one of Miley's music idols. Like Miley, Dolly Parton started singing at a young age. In fact, before she could even read or write, Dolly was making up her own songs. She got her first guitar when she was eight and by eleven she was singing on a radio station in Knoxville, Tennessee. As soon as she graduated from high school, Dolly moved to Nashville to start her career. And what a career it was—and still is!

Dolly has had 26 singles that went to number 1 on the charts (a record for a female performer), and a record 42 Top 10 Country albums. Dolly also performed on a Top 40 country hit in each of the last five decades. Miley must be very inspired by Dolly's success, and she was absolutely thrilled when this music idol guest-starred on an episode of *Hannah Montana*!

Miley likes country music but she also likes pop, and one of her pop idols is Kelly Clarkson. Kelly was the winner on the first season of the popular reality television show *American Idol*. After nabbing the top prize on that show, Kelly signed with RCA records and released her debut album, *Thankful*. Kelly's second album, *Breakaway*, went multi-platinum and also showcased more of a pop-rock style of music. On June 26, 2007, Kelly released her third album, *My December*. Eight of Kelly's singles were top 10 hits on Billboard's Hot 100 chart. Miley is probably very inspired by Kelly's rise to fame, but also knows that this successful *American Idol* alumna had to work hard to get there.

Miley's musical taste also includes pop punk, as

evidenced by her love of the band Paramore. Hailing from Miley's hometown of Franklin, Tennessee, this quartet is quickly becoming huge in the music world. The band is made up of vocalist Haley Williams, Jeremy Davis on the bass, and brothers Joshua and Zachary Farro (Josh plays the guitar, and Zac plays the drums). Haley, Josh, and Zac all met in school, and discovered they shared a love of music. They formed Paramore in 2004, after adding Jeremy to the group. They played their first show in Nashville, and quickly gained a loyal following, including Miley! Their big break happened in 2005 when Fueled By Ramen founder John Janick saw them playing in Florida. Janick was blown away by Paramore and signed the band to his label. Paramore's debut album, *All We Know is Falling* created a buzz in the music industry. The group hit the road in 2006 and toured nonstop through North America, Europe, and Japan. In 2007, the band released their second album, *Riot*, which went platinum. Paramore's popularity continued to grow, but what probably gave them their biggest commercial boost was having two of their singles, "Decode" and "I Caught Myself" featured on the sound track for the hugely popular *Twilight* movie. Miley must be very proud that a band from her hometown has made it so big!

Besides country, pop rock, and pop punk, Miley has been influenced by R&B. Beyoncé Knowles, an R&B singer and songwriter, is another artist who has inspired Miley Cyrus. Born in Houston, Texas, Beyoncé was hooked on music from an early age. She attended performing arts schools, and took part in singing and dancing competitions. Beyoncé's rise to fame came in the late 1990s when she was the lead singer for the group Destiny's Child, which is the best-selling girl group of all time. Beyoncé saw success with the group, but she also wanted to break out on her own. In 2003, she released her solo album *Dangerously in Love*, and it was a huge hit, earning her five Grammys. Beyoncé released her second album, *B'Day*, in 2006 and her third album, *I Am . . . Sasha*

Fierce, in 2008. All in all, Beyonce has sold over 63 million albums worldwide. Beyoncé has also become a bona fide movie star, with starring roles in *The Pink Panther* and *Dreamgirls*.

Looking at Beyoncé's career, you can see a lot of similarities with the path Miley has taken so far. Both Beyoncé and Miley broke out on their own, and both have made it on the big screen. It is clear that Miley has taken something from all of her musical influences to make her the star she is today!

Chapter 21

A Perfect Five

Miley is probably number one on your list of favorite stars. And if you had to rate her on a scale of one to ten, you'd most definitely give her a perfect ten. So you'd probably be surprised to hear that Miley's actually a five, at least according to numerology.

Numerology is a practice built on the statement of the ancient Greek philosopher Pythagoras who said, "The world is built upon the power of numbers." According to this theory, all things, including names, can be reduced down to a number in order to figure out personalities, destinies, and fortunes of individuals.

According to numerology, each person's personality fits into one of nine categories. In order to figure out someone's number, you have to match up each letter in his or her name to a particular number on a numerology chart.

How did we figure out that Miley is a five? First we wrote out all the letters in Miley's full name. But there's a catch here: You need to use the name that is written on your birth certificate. Destiny Hope Cyrus is on Miley's birth certificate, but since she *legally* changed her name, we used Miley Ray. Then we matched the letters to the numbers on this chart:

1	2	3	4	5	6	7	8	9
A	B	C	D	E	F	G	H	I
J	K	L	M	N	O	P	Q	R
S	T	U	V	W	X	Y	Z	

First, let's add up the numbers in MILEY: 4 + 9 + 3 + 5 + 7 = 28. Next, we have to get the 28 down to a single digit, so we add up 2 + 8 to get 10. Then add up 1+0 to get 1. Remember that number.

Next, let's look at RAY: 9 + 1 + 7 = 17. To get 17 to a single digit, add 1 + 7 to get 8. Remember that number.

Finally, let's add up CYRUS: 3 + 7 + 9 + 3 + 1 = 23. To get 23 to a single digit, add 2 + 3 to get 5. Remember that number.

Now let's add up the three numbers you remembered: 1 + 8 + 5 = 14. To get 14 to a single digit add 1 + 4 to get 5. That's the answer! Miley is a 5 on the numerology chart. But what does that mean?

It means that number five fits Miley perfectly! Fives are multi-talented and versatile. They can do many things well. That is a great description of Miley. She's a pop star, a TV star, *and* a movie star. And being able to jockey back and forth between Hannah Montana and Miley Cyrus proves that she's versatile! And like a true number five, Miley is able to easily adapt to change.

As a number five, Miley is good at presenting ideas, and knowing how to get what she wants, although she can't always talk her way out of being grounded! A lot of number fives end up in the entertainment business, which is exactly where Miley has landed.

Fives love adventure and are constantly moving. Sometimes this trait leads to restlessness, and fives have a hard time following a routine. But this characteristic suits Miley well, since her schedule is always changing!

You can figure out your own numerology, too. Just add up the letters in your name. Who knows? Maybe you and Miley are numerological twins!

Number **ones** are extremely self-confident, self-reliant, and disciplined. When someone has self-discipline, they are able to correct or regulate themselves in order to improve upon what they have been doing. Number ones also make great leaders. People who are number ones are creative, independent, and original. Although number ones can be very generous, they have to be careful not to become too self-obsessed.

A number **two** is almost the complete opposite of a number one. They are not interested in becoming leaders. They are fair and always look at both sides of a situation before jumping to a conclusion. Twos are very gentle and patient and supportive of others, and they are able to easily empathize with other people's situations. Twos have to be careful not to let others take advantage of them.

Threes are very enthusiastic. They have a good sense of humor and are always ready to party. Threes are charming, creative, and very friendly. However, threes can sometimes have a sharp tongue, so they have to be careful not to hurt others feelings.

Fours are very practical and orderly people. They are hard workers who take their responsibilities very seriously. They are steadfast and often set in their ways, which could get them into trouble. Fours sometimes need to learn to be more flexible.

Fives love adventure and are always on the go. They love to explore, and their curiosity leads them to new places. People who are fives are never satisfied with the status quo; they crave change. Fives often start many different projects but don't always finish them since they are constantly looking for something new to do.

Sixes are very nurturing people. Sixes are very loving, kind, and gentle. They are full of understanding and see beauty in life. Since a lot of their decisions come from the heart, it can be difficult to reason with sixes.

Sevens often make great teachers. They are wise and deep thinkers. Sevens are loners, and can be quite reserved. People who are sevens have to be careful not to withdraw from society too much.

People who are **eights** are born leaders who are high achievers and who are successful. Sometimes eights hold grudges, so they need to learn to forgive and forget.

Nines are very compassionate. They are always helping others in need. People who are nines are very loving and generous. They are also extremely charming! However, they need to be careful not to force their beliefs on others who think differently.

Chapter 22

A New Name

Destiny. Hope. Miley. Ray. Hannah. So many names for just one girl. Although Miley doesn't use Destiny Hope anymore, Miley's parents named her Destiny because they thought she was destined for greatness—and they were right. Here's a look at what Miley's given names mean:

Name: Destiny

Gender: Female

Origin: English

Meaning: This name has the same meaning as the noun *destiny*—something that has been decided beforehand. It can also mean *fate*—something that is unavoidable.

Name: Hope

Gender: Female

Origin: English

Meaning: The name has the same meaning as the noun or verb *hope*—to desire something and expect that it will happen or that you will be able to get it.

Name: Ray

Gender: Male

Origin: English

Meaning: This name means wise protector. Miley "adopted" this name from her dad. With this name she probably feels as if her dad is always protecting her.

Even though Miley plays a character named Hannah on TV, lots of fans call her Hannah when they see her. But Miley doesn't mind. Here's a look at what the name Hannah means:

Name: Hannah

Gender: Female

Origin: Hebrew, English, French, German

Meaning: From the Hebrew name Channah, which means favor or grace. In the Torah (Hebrew Bible), Hannah was the mother of Samuel the prophet. The Latin version of this name is Anna.

Billy Ray gave Miley her nickname when she was a baby—it was shortened from Smiley. So Miley isn't a real name, right? Well, sort of. Miley is actually an Irish family name. It was derived from the word *muadh*, which has three meanings: noble and big and soft. Maybe noble could be used to describe Miley, but big and soft? Not so much!

Chapter 23

Pop Star

There's no doubt about it—Miley Cyrus is a bona fide pop star. Some may think that the reason the *Hannah Montana* CD debuted at number 1 on the charts was due solely to the popularity of the TV show. This was *so* not the case. The CD has many merits of its own, which cannot be denied. The CD features well-written songs that give nods to teen pop, rock, and country. The themes of having fun, being yourself, and following your dreams that are found throughout the album speak directly to tweens and teens. And Miley's rich voice is infused with such personality! After listening to the CD once, you'll find yourself humming the tunes and singing the lyrics in the shower.

Miley, as Hannah, sings eight of the tracks. Also

featured on the CD are the Click Five, Jesse McCartney, Everlife, and B5. On the last track, Miley sings a song as herself—a duet with her dad, Billy Ray.

Hannah Montana discography:

1. "The Best of Both Worlds"—Hannah Montana
2. "Who Said"—Hannah Montana
3. "Just Like You"—Hannah Montana
4. "Pumpin' Up the Party"—Hannah Montana
5. "If We Were a Movie"—Hannah Montana
6. "I Got Nerve"—Hannah Montana
7. "The Other Side of Me"—Hannah Montana
8. "This Is the Life"—Hannah Montana
9. "Pop Princess"—The Click Five
10. "She's No You"—Jesse McCartney
11. "Find Yourself in You"—Everlife
12. "Shining Star"—B5
13. "I Learned from You"—Miley Cyrus and Billy Ray Cyrus

There is also a special edition of the sound track that has two discs. The first disc is the standard CD with thirteen songs. The second disc is a DVD with five music videos used in the show:

1. "The Best of Both Worlds"
2. "Who Said"
3. "Just Like You"
4. "Pumpin' Up the Party"
5. "The Other Side of Me"

When Miley's second CD came out, she was showing the world that she was both Hannah Montana and Miley Cyrus. Here's what you can hear on this two disc collection:

Hannah Montana 2: Meet Miley Cyrus discography:

Disc 1:

1. "We Got the Party"
2. "Nobody's Perfect"

3. “Make Some Noise”
4. “Rock Star”
5. “Old Blue Jeans”
6. “Life’s What You Make It”
7. “One in a Million”
8. “Bigger Than Us”
9. “You and Me Together”
10. “True Friend”

Disc 2:

1. “See You Again”
2. “East Northumberland High”
3. “Let’s Dance”
4. “G.N.O.” (Girl’s Night Out)
5. “Right Here”
6. “As I Am”
7. “Start All Over”
8. “Clear”
9. “Good and Broken”

10. "I Miss You"

Breakout is all Miley. Here's what you can rock out to:

1. "Breakout"
2. "7 Things"
3. "The Driveway"
4. "Girls Just Wanna Have Fun"
5. "Full Circle"
6. "Fly on the Wall"
7. "Bottom of the Ocean"
8. "Wake Up America"
9. "These Four Walls"
10. "Simple Song"
11. "Goodbye"
12. "See You Again"

Chapter 24

Fifty Fast Facts

You're Miley's biggest fan. Here's everything you need to know about her, right at your fingertips:

1. **Given name:** Destiny Hope Cyrus
2. **Nicknames:** Miley, Home G, Milo
3. **How she got her nickname:** As a baby, Miley was always smiling, so her dad called her Smiley, which was later shortened to Miley
4. **Alter ego:** Hannah Montana
5. **Birthday:** November 23, 1992
6. **Sign:** Sagittarius
7. **Hometown:** Franklin, Tennessee
8. **Present home:** Los Angeles, California

9. **Hair color:** Brown
10. **Wig color:** Blond
11. **Eye color:** Blue/green
12. **Height:** 5'4"
13. **Father:** Billy Ray Cyrus
14. **Mother:** Leticia "Tish" Cyrus
15. **Siblings:** Older half brothers, Christopher and Trace; older half sister, Brandi; younger brother, Braison; and younger sister, Noah Lindsey
16. **Pets:** Miley has a dog named Loco that's with her in California, and a new puppy named Sophie. But back in Tennessee, she has seven horses, three dogs, and two cats.
17. **First time singing onstage:** When Miley was two, she was onstage singing with her dad.
18. **First TV role:** Kylie on the PAX show *Doc*

19. **First movie role:** Ruthie in Tim Burton's *Big Fish*

20. **Fave spots on the *Hannah Montana* set:** Her dressing room and the beach

21. **Posters on her dressing room wall:** Orlando Bloom, Keira Knightley, Kelly Clarkson

22. **Favorite sport:** Cheerleading

23. **Hobby:** Shopping!

24. **Jewelry she's never without:** A purple and white bracelet that was a gift from a fan, a bracelet from a water park, and a silver ring that her dad gave her mom

25. **Favorite subjects:** Math and creative writing

26. **Secret #1:** She can't keep a secret!

27. **Secret #2:** Miley has had braces, but they were on the inside of her teeth.

28. **Best bud:** Mandy

29. **Celebrity buds:** Emily Osment, Mitchel Musso, Ashley Tisdale

30. **Best way to keep in touch with her friends:** Using her Sidekick

31. **Musical influence:** Kelly Clarkson

32. **Idols:** Kelly Clarkson, Raven-Symoné, Judge Judy

33. **Favorite TV show:** *Laguna Beach*

34. **Favorite movie:** *Steel Magnolias*

35. **Favorite actress:** Sandra Bullock

36. **Favorite book:** *Don't Die, My Love* by Lurlene McDaniel

37. **Musical instrument:** Miley learned to play the guitar a few years ago. She was given a Daisy Rock guitar by her parents.

38. **Celebrity crushes:** Ryan Cabrera, Ashton Kutcher, Orlando Bloom, and Chad Michael Murray

39. **Comfy item on tour bus:** Elvis blanket

40. **Candy she likes to eat:** Gummy bears

41. **Type of food she likes to eat:** Fast food, shrimp

42. **Favorite condiment:** Ketchup

43. **Favorite snack:** Cookie dough

44. **Favorite cookie:** Sugar cookie

45. **Favorite drink:** Caramel Frappuccinos

46. **Five songs on Miley's iPod:** "Beating Hearts Baby" by Head Automatica, "California" by Copeland, "Invisible" by Ashlee Simpson, "Please Be Mine" by Jonas Brothers, and "It's Going Down" by Yung Joc

47. **Bands Miley digs:** Underoath, Copeland, They Said We Were Ghosts, Paramore

48. **Favorite thing to do when she's not working (or shopping):** Curl up and watch a video with little sis, Noah

49. **What Miley put in a time capsule:** A picture of Beyoncé, because she wants to have a career like hers, and a picture of a dress that she wants

50. **Future recording contract:** A four-record deal with Hollywood Records

Chapter 25

Pop Quiz

Now you know absolutely everything about Miley Cyrus, right? Okay then, it's pop quiz time! (And no turning back pages to find the answers!)

1. What is the name of Miley's new dog?

- **a.** Sydney
- **b.** Loco
- **c.** Sophie
- **d.** Lenny

2. Which charity did Miley help support with proceeds from her concert?

- **a.** City of Angels
- **b.** City Hospital

c. City of Hope

d. City of Children

3. What color is Miley's Daisy Rock guitar?

a. Pink

b. Electric blue

c. Fuchsia

4. What is Miley's little sister's name?

a. Noa Lizzie

b. Noah Lindsey

c. Nikki Lesley

5. What's the name of Miley's hometown?

a. Franklin

b. Flatwoods

c. Francis

6. Which awards ceremony did Miley host?

- **a.** Oscars
- **b.** Teen Choice
- **c.** Grammys
- **d.** Emmys

7. What word would Miley use to describe herself?

- **a.** quiet
- **b.** studious
- **c.** giggly
- **d.** neat

8. What is something that Miley wants to do before her life is over?

- **a.** Become a teacher
- **b.** Swim in the Red Sea
- **c.** Skydive
- **d.** Climb Mount Everest

9. On which CD is the song "Simple Song"?

a. Meet Miley Cyrus

b. Hannah Montana 2

c. Breakout

d. Hannah Montana

10. Who has Miley signed a recording deal with?

a. Hollywood Records

b. Mercury Records

c. Sony

d. Warner

Answers: 1. c, 2. c, 3. a, 4. b, 5. a, 6. b, 7. c, 8. b, 9. c, 10. a

Chapter 26

Miley Mania

In case you haven't been able to catch Miley in person, you can always find her if you flip through a teen mag—and lots of times she's on the cover! You can also catch up on what Miley's been doing by surfing the Net. But a word of caution here: Always be careful when you're online. Never give out any kind of personal information—like your name, address, the name of the school you go to, the name of your sport's team. And never, ever set up a meeting with someone you meet online. Downloading pictures from an unknown source is another no-no.

When you're surfing the Net, you have to remember that not everything you read is true. It's smart to take in all the info with a grain of salt. There are lots of people creating websites out there, and some of their information can be exactly that: created. Before you go online, get permission from a parent or another adult in your home. And remember, websites are constantly coming and going, so if your favorite one disappears, don't worry—there will be another one to take its place!

Miley Cyrus Official Site

www.mileycyrus.com

Miley Cyrus Tribute—a fan site

www.mileyworld.com

Miley Fans

www.mileyfans.net

Hannah Montana Official Site

tv.disney.go.com/disneychannel/hannahmontana/index.html

Chapter 27

What's Next

Who is Miley Cyrus? She is a teenager, who with virtually no professional acting experience is the star of one of the hottest shows on Disney. She is a teenager, who, with a limited singing and performing résumé has three best-selling CDs, and a record-smashing concert and movie. At first, her accomplishments were based off *Hannah Montana*. But then Miley Cyrus broke out as a super talented star in her own right. "I love doing it all," Miley told *Variety*. "When I'm doing one thing, I always miss the other. When I'm on tour, I miss shooting the show and I miss the cast. When I'm shooting the show, I miss doing concerts and performing my music for all of my fans." It seems as if Miley Cyrus is truly stuck between two worlds!

What's ahead for Miley? Well, she has more albums ahead with Hollywood Records—she signed a four-record deal. And with new albums, new concert tours are definitely in Miley's future. As far as *Hannah Montana* goes, despite rumors that she was ready to leave the show, Miley told *People* that "I am fully committed to *Hannah Montana*. It's what gave me this amazing opportunity to reach out to so many people. I couldn't do it alone. We have an amazing cast that is so supportive, including my dad who has been there for me every step of the way." Miley has a contractual obligation to film a third and fourth season of the hit show.

Using her role as Hannah Montana, Miley bulked up the "movie star" portion of her resume when she stared in *Hannah Montana: The Movie* in 2009. "This is not a two-hour version of what you might be able to see on Disney Channel," Adam Bonnett, senior VP of original programming for the network told *Variety*. That was certainly clear to movie goers, who saw the location of the show change from Malibu to Nashville, and saw that Miley had a new love interest in the movie.

Miley got some very exciting movie news when Disney announced that she was to star in an untitled film that is being tailor-made by author Nicholas Sparks. Sparks is writing a novel and a screenplay adaptation of the film, which will be produced by Disney-affiliated Offspring partners Adam Shankman and Jennifer Gibgot. According to *Variety*, Miley's mom Tish will be an executive producer.

Nicholas Sparks is well known for his novel and movie, *The Notebook*, as well as *A Walk to Remember*, which moved Mandy Moore from pop star to movie star. Sparks has an idea for Miley's movie, which he has shared with Miley and her family, but is not letting the public in on it yet. The book will be published in fall 2009 by Grand Central Publishing. In a statement in *Variety*, Sparks said, "This is similar to the way it's gone with movies based on my novels; it's just out of order. Certain opportunities garner your interest, and this was one of those." Sparks said that Miley and her family knew of his work, and that knowledge helped the project come together.

Whether it's being a pop star or a movie star, Miley truly enjoys what she's doing. In an interview with the UK publication *The Times*, Miley said, "I like working a lot then taking a really long break. But it's so funny: every time I get a day off I'm like 'Mom, I need to go to the studio. Mom, I need to write a song.' She's like 'Just take your day off.' But I just like working. I like what I do. So it's good."

With all this good fortune, Miley has been able to stay grounded. She is still the bubbly girl from a farm in Franklin, Tennessee. Through all this, Miley has definitely been able to remain true to herself. Miley loves what she does, but she also knows that it's her fans that got her where she is today, and keep her on top. "For me it's all about the love of acting and the love of music," she told *The Times*. "But then again, when you see three million, four million, five million pop up on your screen (when watching the rating numbers) . . . that's pretty insane. 'Cause it wasn't like I got an easy free ride."

It is certainly true that Miley didn't have a free and easy ride to the top. But from the looks of it, the top is where Miley Cyrus is going to stay!

Check out these other hot stars!